The *Price* Of *Freedom*

The Price Of Freedom

DEBRA J BRIGHT

Kravitz & Sons

INNOVATORS IN PUBLISHING, MARKETING AND ADVERTISING

Kravitz and Sons LLC
204 E Arlington Blvd. Suite B
Greenville, NC 27858

Published by Kravitz and Sons LLC.

ISBN: 979-8-89639-457-0 (sc)
ISBN: 979-8-89639-456-3 (e)

Library of Congress Control Number: 2026902316

Table Of Contents

Acknowledgement

I would like to extend my heartfelt thanks to **Curtis Bright, Yolanda Wilkinson**, and **Milton Dohoney** for their literary contributions to *The Price of Freedom*. Your insight, creativity, and dedication added depth and meaning to this story. I am deeply grateful for your collaboration and the thoughtful energy you brought to this work.

To everyone who encouraged me along the way—thank you for believing in this story and in the message it carries. Your support has been constant reminder that freedom begins with awareness, compassion, and courage.

Preface

—◦◦◦—

Have you ever wondered what the United States would look like today if Abraham Lincoln had lost the presidential election and slavery was never abolished?

After Lincoln, other presidents tried but failed to end slavery. The government argued that abolishing slavery would destroy the nation's economy, since it was the foundation on which the country was built. Instead of ending it, the government expanded and refined the system, financially and socially.

Slavery was abolished everywhere in the world, except the United States. The reason was simple: greed. By the turn of the century, slavery had spread from the South to the rest of the states. The North saw how wealthy the South had become, with fortunes greater than those of most nations, and many of the world's richest people lived in the southern states because of slavery.

Now let's look at the United States in the year 2030. The nation consists of 48 states bordered by Canada, the Atlantic Ocean, Mexico, and the Pacific Ocean. It is the fourth-largest country in the world, after Russia, Canada, and China. The capital is Washington, D.C.

The United States is the world's greatest economic power, its wealth drawn from natural resources, agriculture, industry, and most importantly, slavery. Population is concentrated in major cities such as New York, Los Angeles, Chicago, and Miami.

New York City, with a population of about 10 million, is the nation's largest and wealthiest city. It leads in factory production, banking, and financial services, and is also a center for the arts, theater, and fashion.

Los Angeles has over 5 million residents. Its neighborhoods are divided into districts for the arts, government, fashion, banking, theater, shopping, and film.

Miami, with a population of more than 800,000, is one of the largest cities in the South. Its second-largest population is Hispanic and Latino. Miami is also a leader in finance, commerce, and international trade.

The U.S. population consists largely of whites, but an even greater share are slaves. A small minority are free Blacks, often freed by their masters, sometimes because they were their children. But their freedom is limited. They face discrimination and restrictions: they cannot dine in the same restaurants, attend the same schools, or share public spaces with whites. Still, free Blacks can vote, own property, pursue education, travel, and organize.

Some enslaved families have managed to save money over generations, hoping one day their descendants could buy their freedom. Most knew they would never live to see freedom themselves.

Over time, slave owners recognized the intelligence of their slaves and turned it to their advantage. Once it was illegal to teach slaves to read or write, but now they are allowed, encouraged, even, to pursue education, since it benefits their masters. The more educated they are, the higher their social standing and the more valuable they become. Slaves are now ranked in classes according to intelligence, education, and profession:

- Class 5 – Doctors, Scientists, Executives, Engineers
- Class 4 – Professors, Nurses, Teachers, Managers
- Class 3 – Manufacturing, Farmers, Construction Workers
- Class 2 – Sales Clerks, Waiters, Child Care Providers, Janitors (Service Providers)
- Class 1 – Organ Donors, Research Participants, Test Subjects, or whatever the Master sees fit (within the law)

No slave wants to be Class 1, for obvious reasons. Everyone strives for higher status, but many remain trapped in their class, either by limited ability or because their master holds them there. Poor masters often own only a few slaves and lack the resources to educate them, while some simply do not care about long-term investment.

Classes are easy to recognize in public by the color of garments slaves are required to wear: Class 5 wears black, Class 4 white, Class 3 orange, Class 2 red, Class 1 green, and all students gray. This system makes it clear what work they do and where they belong in society.

All slaves are required to work five days a week, ten hours a day. They are paid, but 50% of their salary goes to their master. In today's society, slaves need income to survive and support their families. They have weekends off, though they must remain available if called by their master, unless they hold a weekend job, which requires permission. Some choose extra work to keep the money earned on days off, since it does not have to be shared. Slaves assigned to plantation jobs cannot work outside the plantation and are not allowed to travel beyond their region without permission.

Slaves are not required to live on plantations unless their duties are there, such as maids, cooks, butlers, mechanics, or gardeners. Those who live off plantations must reside in segregated neighborhoods nearby.

The white population's constant desire for wealth has driven the need for more slaves, and the slave population now outnumbers whites by millions. The United States has about 650 million people, of whom nearly 500 million are slaves and free Blacks. With the population and value of slaves growing, the government devised new, more "humane" ways of managing them through laws and technology.

In the past, slaves endured whipping, shackling, beating, mutilation, branding, rape, and hanging. Families were torn apart through sales, never to reunite. Family separations still occur, but now through a legal process. Present-day laws forbid certain abuses: masters can face heavy fines or even prison for inhumane treatment, and the government monitors slave welfare.

Technology plays a central role. Masters track slaves through implanted devices that can deliver electric shocks as punishment. Newborns are implanted at birth, and at age sixteen the chips are replaced with stronger versions. Introduced in 1991 to stop runaway slaves, these devices send shocks if a slave leaves their region or disobeys orders, and they can render the slave incapacitated until retrieved. Cameras and drones further track their movements.

My story follows a slave family living in Washington, D.C., navigating daily life in 2030.

Gabriel Brown is married and the father of four. He is tall, slim, and brown-skinned, with thick black hair, a close-cut beard, and dark eyes. He works as an aerospace engineer developing defense technologies. His wife, Jesse, is a medical doctor who designed new medical chips. Because of their careers, they are at the top of Class 5, each earning about $150,000, half of which goes to Master Brown. Even so, they live comfortably by slave standards and are his most valuable family.

Their four children show equal promise.

Hope, 23, is a graduate student training to be a doctor. Tall and slim like her father, with her mother's light skin, hazel eyes, and long black hair, she is striking but tries to downplay her looks, fearing the attention of masters. Her dream is to live in Paris as a free woman. After graduation, she plans to work, save money, and buy her freedom through an underground group that helps slaves escape. She will move back in with her parents in the meantime.

Destinee, 15, is bright but struggles with anger issues. Constantly fighting in school, she has already been warned multiple times. Her parents fear her behavior will draw punishment from their master.

Samuel and Seth, 10-year-old twins, are inseparable. They spend their time playing, laughing, and pulling harmless tricks on their sisters.

Chapter 1
Jesse's Day at Work

Today is just a typical day. Gabriel is getting dressed for work; Jesse is preparing breakfast before leaving for the hospital. The kids are at the table when Gabriel runs downstairs. Jesse hands him a sandwich. "Here, you can't be late." Gabriel grabs it, kisses her on the cheek, and runs out the door. Jesse claps; the kids know what that means and run out after him. Jesse grabs her briefcase and rushes out as well, realizing she's late. She'll text Master to let him know so the hospital doesn't contact him.

Jesse parks her small white compact, the color matches her classification, and arrives at the hospital with thirty seconds to spare. She's relieved she's working on the second floor today; if she were on the fifteenth, where she usually works, she would have been late. She's assigned to the delivery room and helped design a new location chip to implant in newborns. These won't need replacing until they turn sixteen, when they'll receive stronger chips along with discipline chips.

Jesse hates the chips she helped create, but they're much better than the ankle bracelets used before. Those bracelets were worn even by infants and had to be changed every few months as children outgrew them. Slave owners liked the chips because they only had to be replaced once, at sixteen; it saved them money.

Jesse is working with Lorretta today. She likes Lorretta; it makes the day go faster. Lorretta is in her mid-sixties with a wild sense of humor. Jesse laughs the whole day away with her. Lorretta trained Jesse for this job, and they've been close ever since; Lorretta is like a mother to her.

Jesse is concerned about the chips being implanted in newborns. She thinks they should be removed by age six; she believes it's unsafe to keep them past that, but nobody's listening; they're looking at cost. Lorretta snaps, "If it were their white babies in danger, they'd remove

1

them quick." Thousands of kids have died because of these chips, but since many of those children haven't yet shown their value, the owners aren't as concerned.

They put their concerns aside and get on with their responsibilities, ten more hours to go.

Suddenly Jesse and Lorretta are called to the emergency room. They run in and are met by a room full of children: crying, convulsing, blood pouring from their mouths and ears.

Lorretta yells, "What the hell?"

"It's those damn chips," Jesse responds.

A little girl reaches up and grabs Jesse's hand. "Help me, please."

Jesse rolls the girl into an empty area, grabs a surgical knife, and removes the chip from her arm. "It's the chips; remove the chips, hurry!" she tells the other OR staff. Everyone begins removing chips as quickly as possible; they'll worry about suturing later. An hour passes and the last chip is out. They prepare to stitch up the children and send them to recovery.

Meanwhile, parents and Masters fill the waiting room. The Masters are angry, demanding to know why the chips were removed. Jesse explains to the hospital administrator.

"I didn't have a choice. It was the only way to save their lives. If I hadn't ordered the removals, we'd have an emergency room full of dead children." She tells them the chips had expired and should have been replaced.

"There are going to be more incidents like this. We only lost three this time, but there will be more deaths," the administrator warns.

"Well, when the children recover, make sure you implant new chips before they're discharged."

"Yes, sir. I will."

Chapter 2
Gabriel is introduced to the Underground

Gabriel is an aerospace engineer for the federal government in design, research, and development. He is one of the top engineers at his firm, working alongside the best in Washington, D.C.

James, an engineering manager, leans over Gabriel's cubicle.

"Hey Gabriel, you really know your stuff."

Gabriel smiles. "Aw, I'm alright, but thanks."

"I'm having a little get-together tonight, drinks, poker. You should come by. I'd like you to meet some of the guys. Just tell your Master it's a work meeting," James says with a wink.

"I'll try to make it," Gabriel replies with a smile.

James heads to his office, makes a call, and says, "He'll be there," before hanging up.

The day passes quickly, and before Gabriel knows it, it's 7:00. James stops by on his way out.

"Don't forget tonight. I know you said you'd try, but it's important. I need to talk to you about something, and here isn't the place. Be at my house at 8:30. I'll text you the address."

Gabriel calls Jesse to say he'll be late, then drives to James's house, wondering what's so important. James has never invited him over before, especially since Gabriel is a free man. Free men usually socialize with each other. He'll soon find out.

Arriving at James's house, Gabriel notices a drone overhead as he walks to the door. He rings the bell. James answers.

"Come on in, I'm glad you made it."

James leads him to the basement, where Gabriel is greeted by four Black men and one white man, unusual and unsettling.

Seeing his unease, James says, "Gabriel, I'll explain. That's why I invited you. First, have a drink and relax." He gestures for Gabriel to sit.

"Gabriel, we're members of an organization called the Underground. You've heard of the Underground Railroad, haven't you? This is an extension of that. It's grown into a nationwide secret network that not only helps slaves escape but also helps them adjust to freedom. Some we help for nothing, others we charge depending on the risk and distance.

"We have routes to Mexico, South America, and Canada. Escapes require fake passports, visas, birth certificates, and other documents. We even have planes and ships to get people to Europe, Africa, Australia, but those are costly. They're owned by wealthy white abolitionists who back our cause.

"Some families have been saving for generations, passing money down so their descendants could one day be free. They knew they might never see freedom themselves, but their children or grandchildren would. That's why our work is bigger than just crossing into Canada like in the old days.

"Our organization is run by freed slaves who vowed to help as many others as possible, along with white abolitionists, some descended from the originals. Gabriel, I'm one of them. I'm a descendant of Gertie Davis, Harriet Tubman's adoptive daughter. I was born into this organization, fourth generation Underground. This is all I know, and if things don't change, I'll pass the torch to my children."

"As you plan?"

"Yes, as we plan."

James looks around the room. "Gabriel, we'd like you to join us. I've been watching you, waiting for the right time, and we've decided that time is now."

"But I'm not free," Gabriel replies.

"I know. But you're one of the smartest men I know, at the top of your field. We need people like you. We can work around the fact that you're not free yet."

"Need me for what? I'm a slave. I don't have the freedom to move like you do."

"Like I said, we can work around that. But here's why we need you: for your intelligence. And maybe even your wife's expertise."

"My wife?"

"Yes. Only if necessary. She's a doctor, and she helped design the chips. If our first plan fails, we may need her." James pauses, then leans in. "What I'm about to tell you stays with you. Not even your wife can know. Lives depend on your silence. Can we trust you?"

"You can trust me."

James nods. "Our plan is to get one of us into the White House. A man who will guarantee freedom for all. This country was built by us, our blood, sweat, and tears. Why should we leave what we built? Our ancestors' blood is in this soil. I'll be damned if I leave it."

The men cheer, voices rising in agreement. Leaving was never an option. This is their country, their ancestors' land.

"Gabriel, the man you've been glancing at, he's not white. He's mulatto. His name is Anthony Hamilton, and he's going to be the next President of the United States, if all goes as we plan."

James continues, "We outnumber them. We could take our country back, if not for those damn chips. Any attempt at revolt, and they push a button, and it's over. We've spent years trying to find the facility that controls the chips so we can destroy it.

"Here's the plan: Whites will vote for Anthony because they'll think he's a white man from a political family. Free Blacks will vote for him because they know the truth. Once he's in office, he'll work to abolish slavery. And when slavery falls, the chips will be deactivated or removed."

James takes a breath. "But if abolition fails, we have a backup. A team is already searching for the facility that controls the towers transmitting signals to the chips. Once they find it, we'll destroy it.

When the chips are dead, slaves can't be controlled. They'll be free. This is where you and your wife come in; she helped design them. She can help destroy them."

He looks Gabriel square in the eye. "Every other country abolished slavery in the 1800s. But here, greed rules. This land was built by slaves. Millions died building it. My family could have left many times, but why should we? This is our country. I will not leave. I will stay until it is free, and I will see it in my lifetime."

James extends his hand. "Help us, Gabriel. Help us free our people."

Gabriel looks around at the faces in the room, then back at James.

"I'm with you," he says.

The men gather around him, shaking his hand, patting his back, welcoming him into their cause. James introduces him to Anthony Hamilton, the future President of the United States.

"Thank you for joining us, Gabriel," Anthony says. "We still have a long way to go, but we'll get there. And with you, we're already closer."

Chapter 3
Hope, The Dreamer

—◦◦◦—

Hope is awakened by the sun shining on her face through the blinds she left open last night. She likes to lie in bed looking up at the stars, waiting for a shooting star to wish upon, a wish to live as a free woman in her favorite city, Paris, France. She has always dreamed of living there, a dream she is determined to make come true.

She glances over to see if her roommate is still asleep. They both have an 8:00 class to get to. She throws her pillow at her.

"Get up, girl. We've got to hit the showers."

"I'm coming, I'm coming," her roommate mumbles.

Hope is in her last semester as a graduate student at the University. Becoming a doctor has been her dream since childhood, when her mother used to bring her to work. Maintaining a 4.0 GPA was required, and she never fell below it. This made her as valuable as her parents, following in their footsteps of intelligence and holding a Class 5 status. She once thought if she kept that status, she could raise money faster and buy her freedom. But she soon realized the more money you bring to your Master, the less likely they'll let you go. You're too valuable. It's a no-win situation. Escaping through the Underground offers a better chance.

Akim, Hope's boyfriend, is also studying to be a doctor. He shares her dream of one day living in Paris or Rome, surrounded by Renaissance art. Akim has a great love for the Renaissance and has become a talented painter himself. His Master discovered his gift when he was only nine years old. Akim would spend all his free time drawing and painting. His Master profited from selling the works but always shared the earnings with Akim, something he didn't have to do. If only he knew what Akim was planning with that money. Between what he's saved from his art and what he and Hope will earn as doctors, they'll have enough to buy their freedom and move to Paris, where they plan to marry.

Hope and Akim have been dating for about a year. Their shared dream of Paris is what first drew them together. But Hope's feelings aren't as strong as Akim's. She knows he loves her deeply, while she tells herself her feelings will grow into the kind of love a marriage requires. For now, she loves him more like a friend. She wonders sometimes if it's the $175,000 he has saved that keeps her there. She hopes not. That kind of money puts freedom within reach, closer to Paris. Few slaves have that kind of fortune. His Master treats him unusually well, even allowing him to keep it. Akim cares for his Master too, almost like family. Hope sometimes wonders if he would even leave. His Master treats him like a son. She once asked Akim if his Master was his father, but he said he didn't know. He's never been told who his father is, though it's clear from his features that he's biracial.

Later, Akim joins Hope in the student center.

"Hey, sweetheart. I have to go home this weekend. My Master is planning an exhibit of my paintings, and I need to be there."

"Another exhibit?"

"Yes. He wants me to paint live for the crowd; some people can't believe a slave could create such work. But babe, the more I paint, the closer we get to freedom. That's my motivation: make the money, buy our freedom, and marry you."

Hope smiles. "Okay. Go ahead."

Chapter 4
Destinee, The Problem Child

Destinee usually rides the bus home from school. She has to watch her little brothers until her parents get home from work. But not today. Destinee got into another fight. She's always struggled with anger, rebellion, and fighting. Master has already warned her parents that if they don't straighten her out, he will. Their warnings haven't made much difference.

Today she was sent to the office, and this time Master was called, just as he had instructed the school to do if she got in trouble again. She sits there waiting for her mother, bracing herself for the usual lecture at school, followed by another at home. But not this time.

A tall, handsome white man with tan skin, black hair, and ice-blue eyes walks in wearing khaki pants and a black polo shirt with the name Brown embroidered on it. Destinee notices him immediately. The name on his shirt catches her eye; it's her last name too, passed down from their masters. He's escorted to the principal's office and stays about ten minutes. When he comes out with the principal, a dark- skinned, bald, heavyset man, he heads straight to Destinee.

"Come on, girl. Let's go."

Destinee peeks up through her messy hair, confused. She's never seen this man before. Her mother usually picks her up, fussing all the way home. She looks at the principal for help but says nothing.

"Go on, girl. He's your Master. Keep your head down."

"He's not my Master. My mother picks me up."

"She's not picking you up this time," the man replies. "I said if there was one more issue, I'd handle it. So here I am. Be glad my father's not here; he'd handle it differently. Now come on."

Destinee slowly rises and follows him.

"Sir… did I get sold?" she asks, tears rolling down her cheeks.

He laughs. "No, you're not sold."

She climbs into the back seat of a shiny red convertible. She's never been in one before. The interior is bright white. The wind blows her hair everywhere, and she tries to hold her ponytail, but it's useless. He watches her in the rearview mirror, amused, then raises the top.

"I'm Master Brown's son," he says. "I'm in charge of you now."

Her tears fall harder. She notices he drives past the turn to her house but stays silent. She isn't allowed to speak unless spoken to.

Seeing her tears in the mirror, he shakes his head. Pretty girl, he thinks. Pitiful she can't stay out of trouble. He catches the fear in her eyes as she realizes they're not going home.

"No, you're not going home," he finally says.

Since he spoke first, she's allowed to answer.

"Mom and Dad will be looking for me. I need to take care of my little brothers."

"You weren't thinking about your little brothers when you were fighting at school, were you?" Master Kisen says evenly. "You've been warned over and over. You just won't listen. So now I'm handling it."

"Master, I'm sorry. I won't fight anymore, I promise."

"It's too late for sorry, Destinee. Just be quiet. We'll be there soon."

He stops at a gate where a guard waves him through, then drives down a long road to a large stone administrative building. He gets out and opens her door.

"Come on."

Destinee steps out, eyes full of tears. She looks around at the white stone buildings, fear rising in her chest. She doesn't know where she is or if she'll see her family again. Now she wishes she'd listened to the warnings. She wonders if her parents even know where she is, or if they'll come for her. But deep down, she knows they won't. They belong to him too. He's the one in control.

Inside, the headmaster greets them. "Come in, sir." He glances at Destinee. "You wait out here."

Once the door closes, Master Kisen explains, "I just want to scare her straight for a few days. No need for her to know that."

The headmaster smiles. "We can accommodate that, sir."

"I'll be back Sunday to pick her up. A couple of days here should get her together. It better."

"Yes, sir. I'll have one of the girls look after her. It gets rough in here."

"That might be exactly what she needs."

Master Kisen walks out without looking at Destinee.

"Sir, don't leave me here! Please!" she cries. He doesn't turn back.

"Will you call my parents?" she asks the headmaster.

"I'll let them know where you are."

Destinee stands in the hall, crying as she watches Master Kisen leave. Her mind races, why didn't she listen to her parents? Will she ever go home?

The headmaster steps out and studies her tear-streaked face. She looks up at him for the first time. He smiles. He's an older black man, about seventy, with gray hair and a full beard.

"Destinee, someone will be here to get you situated. You'll be alright."

"Can I call my parents, just to let them know where I am?"

"No. Your Master will call them. And don't worry about your phone; I have it."

"Is she ready, sir?" asked a heavyset woman with a smile.

"Yes, she's ready. You can take her."

"Come on, young lady. You're in Building A. We need to get you to the showers and into your uniform."

Destinee is led to a small room with a shower and a table. On the table is a bag of toiletries, towels, and a uniform. She steps into the shower and begins to cry. The water mixes with her tears.

There's a knock at the door.

"Come on, girl. Move it. You ain't home; no long showers here."

Destinee steps out and pulls on the drab gray uniform, a size too big for her small frame. She's then led to the cafeteria for dinner. The moment she walks in, she feels every eye on her. Her stomach knots.

"I'm not hungry. I don't feel good," she whispers to the aide.

"Go on and get your food. Everyone feels like that when they first get here. You'll be alright. I'll sit with you; I need to walk you to your room anyway, introduce you to your roommate."

Destinee fixes a plate and sits beside the aide, still feeling the girls' stares. They can tell she doesn't belong, too pretty, with her light brown skin, long wavy hair, the so-called good hair, and hazel eyes. Everyone wonders what could have landed her here.

She tries to eat but can't. The bell rings, ending dinner. As the girls file out, Destinee rises, but the aide grabs her arm.

"Wait. Let them go first."

When the cafeteria clears, the aide nods. "Come on, let's go."

Destinee arrives at her room, a 20x20 space with two beds, small chests at the foot of each, and a TV on the wall. She sits on one bed as the aide hands her a bag of toiletries.

"Thank you," Destinee murmurs.

The door swings open. A slim, dark-skinned girl with sharp brown eyes and a thick, nappy ponytail stands there.

"Destinee, this is your roommate, Mercy. Mercy, this is Destinee." The aide taps Mercy on the shoulder as she leaves. "Look after her, Mercy."

Mercy stares at Destinee for a long moment.

"Get your ass off my bed," she snaps.

Destinee starts to rise, but Mercy smirks.

"I'm kidding. Stay there, that one's mine."

Destinee lies down, facing the wall, and begins to cry again.

Mercy tosses pajamas onto the bed. "Here. Put these on, get comfortable. Let's watch some TV and get acquainted. And stop all that damn crying; it won't help. What got you in here anyway?"

"Fighting," Destinee mutters.

Mercy laughs. "Fighting? You don't look like a fighter to me. We've got plenty of fighters in here, real ones. If that's your thing, you'll have a lot to choose from." She shakes her head, chuckling. "A fighter, my ass."

Chapter 5
Reform School

———◇◇◇———

The boys arrive at an empty house, not unusual; often they come home to an empty house and don't snitch on their sister, but she's usually back by now. They hear a car pull up.

"Oh, Destinee's in trouble now," Samuel says.

The door opens. "Hey, boys," Jesse calls.

"Hi, Mom," they say, exchanging devious smiles.

"What are you two smiling about?"

"You'll see," Samuel says.

Jesse yells for Destinee. When there's no answer she goes upstairs to Destinee's room. Coming back down, she asks the boys, "Where is your sister?"

"Don't know. She wasn't here when we got home."

Jesse calls Destinee's phone; no answer. She calls Gabriel. "When your daughter gets home, she's in trouble. Won't even answer her phone. She's going on punishment for a year; I'm whipping her ass, I'm so tired of this."

"I'm on my way," Gabriel says. "I know where she is. She's all right. Wait till I get home and I'll explain."

Jesse puts dinner on the table, angrier than ever at Destinee but reassured by Gabriel's voice.

Gabriel arrives. Jesse opens the door as he fumbles with his keys. "Okay, where is she?" she asks.

Gabriel motions the boys upstairs to get ready for bed. "We want to know where Destinee is too."

"You do," Gabriel says. "Maybe if you pay attention you won't make the same mistakes she keeps making."

He explains that Master Kisen called about Destinee's fight at school; Kisen checked her in at the reform school and Gabriel picked her up and took her there.

Jesse starts to cry. "What? We told her to stop fighting; this is what we warned her about."

"Stop crying, let me finish," Gabriel interrupts. "He's keeping her there just for the weekend to scare her; she doesn't know that. She'll be back in a couple of days. Hopefully it scares her straight and she comes back with a new attitude. Master Kisen's getting fed up; if she keeps this up, next time reform school might be permanent."

"Can we go see her?" Jesse asks.

"No. Master Kisen checked her in, so he's the only one they'll allow to see her."

"Okay. It's just the weekend. It'll go by fast, then I'm whipping her ass."

The boys sit silently through the whole conversation, relieved she'll be home.

"Good night, Mom. Good night, Dad. Don't worry about us; we'll be good," Seth says.

"Me too," Samuel adds.

"Should we call Hope and let her know?" Jesse asks.

"No," Gabriel says. "She'll be back in a couple of days. Let her focus on her studies; we don't need to worry her."

Chapter 6
New Best Friend

Destinee is jolted awake by the blaring morning alarm, feeling like she just fell asleep. She spent the night tossing on the thin mattress, crying, missing her family, and wondering if she'd ever see them again. She glances over at her roommate, Mercy, wishing this was only a bad dream.

"Come on, grab your clothes and towel. We have to get to the showers."

"I took one last night."

"Well, you're taking another. We only get showers three times a week."

"I don't have a change of clothes."

"Girl, you put on the clothes you got last night. We only get clean ones when we shower. You're in reform school now, no luxuries like home, so get used to it."

Mercy tosses the towel in Destinee's face. "Come on, hurry up."

They walk into the showers. Destinee stops short and Mercy bumps into her.

"What are you doing? Go on, girl."

The shower is a large room with heads in the ceiling and drains beneath each one. Girls stand beneath them, washing.

"There's no stalls," Destinee whispers.

"Stalls? There are no stalls. We all shower together. You better find a head before the water shuts off; you don't want to be stuck soapy. Don't be timid; everyone's got the same thing. The girls will think you're weak and prey on you. But that's right, you like to fight. I forgot. Now go on."

Destinee lays down her towel, grabs her soap, and finds a shower head. A group of girls starts to surround her. Mercy sees it and calls out:

"Damn, she just got here; give her time to breathe."

The girls glance at Mercy, then back off. No one wants to mess with her; she's one of the toughest girls in reform school. That's why the headmaster made her Destinee's roommate; to keep an eye on her and make sure she didn't get hurt. He told Mercy Destinee was only there for a few days.

When Destinee finishes, she reaches for her towel. It's gone.

"What's wrong?" Mercy asks.

"Someone took my clothes and towel."

"Hold on. I'll get them."

Mercy disappears for a couple minutes, then returns with her things.

"Thanks. Who took them?"

"You'll see. I won't always be around. Stop looking so weak. You'll have to be tough in here; you said you like to fight, right? You might have to prove it."

They head to the cafeteria. Passing a table, Destinee spots a girl holding her eye.

"Can you tell who took your things?" Mercy says with a smile.

They get their breakfast and sit down.

Destinee asks how Mercy ended up in reform school. Mercy shares what little she remembers and what she's been told:

Her parents were level-four slaves. Her father was a janitor, her mother a childcare worker. One day while her mother was caring for children at the facility, a white girl wandered off. Mercy's mother begged her to come back, but the child refused, sneering that she didn't have to listen to a slave. She kept walking toward the street and was hit by a car. The girl survived, but injured. Mercy's mother was blamed, even though she explained the child wouldn't obey.

Her master had to pay for the girl's injuries. To recoup the money, he dropped Mercy's mother down three levels, to level one, and sent her to the brothel he owned. She was young, attractive, and would earn him steady income. He didn't care that it meant tearing her from her husband and child. Separating slave families was illegal, but he found a way around it.

Mercy's father, overcome with grief, refused to work. His master dropped him to level one as well and sold him to a research facility, where he eventually died from experiments. With no one to care for Mercy, her master sent her to reform school, hoping she would grow into a profitable adult. He didn't think she'd be intelligent, since her parents weren't, so he had other plans for her future.

"I've been here since I was nine," Mercy finishes. "I'm fifteen now. Same as you."

"I don't know what's going to become of me. I guess it's whatever my Master decides. I might end up at the brothel with my mother." Mercy sighs. "You don't know how lucky you were, and you just threw it away. I wish I had the life you had. Yes, you're a slave, but your life was better than this. Still, as long as you're here, I'll take care of you. Don't worry, I got you."

She smiles, takes Destinee's hand. "Come on, hurry up and eat."

Mercy asks Destinee to tell her about her life. She wants to know what it's like outside those walls; it's been so long. Destinee tells her story up until reform school. They talk through breakfast, class, lunch, class again, dinner, and back in their room. By the end of the day, they're best friends, knowing everything about each other. Mercy loves hearing about Destinee's family and wishes she had one like hers.

Saturday is movie night, but Mercy and Destinee decide to stay in and watch TV. Mercy drifts off to sleep, but Destinee gets up to use the bathroom. Mercy warned her not to go anywhere alone, but she figures she'll be safe; everyone's watching the movie.

As she opens the bathroom door to leave, five girls walk in, including the one Mercy had given a black eye. Destinee reaches for the door, but it's blocked.

"Excuse me," Destinee says.

"You're excused, but you're not going anywhere. Back up," one of the girls sneers, holding the door.

"Where's your bodyguard?" another girl asks, stepping into her face.

"If you mean Mercy; she's in the room."

"You ready?" one asks.

"Ready for what?"

"Ready for this."

A slap stings her cheek. Destinee slaps back. The others rush her, fists and slaps flying from every direction. She tries to fight back but there are too many. After the beatdown, they run out, warning her not to tell. Destinee lies on the floor, crying.

Back in the room, Mercy wakes up and notices she's gone. "Dammit, I told her not to leave without me." She bolts to the bathroom and finds Destinee on the floor.

"Didn't I tell you not to leave the room without me?"

"I had to use the bathroom."

"You should've woken me up. Now look at you." Mercy helps her up and walks her back to their room.

"You don't have to tell me who did this; I already know. I'll take care of it."

"No, let it go. I don't want to keep dealing with these girls. I don't know how long I'll be here, and you can't protect me everywhere I go."

"Stay here while I get the first-aid kit."

Destinee lies on the bed, wondering how she'll survive this place. Is she going to have to fight her way through? Why didn't she listen to her parents?

Mercy returns with the kit and patches her up. "Looks like you're gonna have a black eye, girlie."

"I don't think I like fighting anymore," Destinee says with a weak smile.

"What? Says the girl who landed in reform school for fighting? You just haven't fought kids like this, angry kids."

"I know. If I could do it over, I'd be good. No more fights. I just want to go home, Mercy."

"Destinee, I have something to tell you. I'm not supposed to, so keep your mouth shut, or me and you will be fighting, and I'll black your other eye."

"What is it? I promise I won't say anything."

"You're going home tomorrow. Your Master brought you here to scare you straight. I was supposed to scare you too, but I couldn't, I liked you from the start. You're getting another chance. Don't screw it up. Try to do better. I don't want you to throw your life away and end up here. I'll miss you. It'd be nice if you could stay, but I wouldn't wish this life on anyone, especially not you. Maybe you can visit me when you're out. I'd love that. I've never had a visitor before."

"Mercy, I promise, I'll never come back here, except to visit you."

They hug, and Destinee shows Mercy how to pinky swear.

Destinee is overjoyed knowing she's going home, though she'll miss her new best friend. The bruises don't hurt as much now, knowing tomorrow she'll be free.

"Mercy?"

"Yes?"

"I'm going to miss you."

"I'm going to miss you too, Destinee."

They fall asleep; Destinee with a smile, Mercy with tears in her eyes.

Chapter 7
Akim

It's Friday, and school is out for the weekend. Hope decides to go home; she hasn't seen her family in a couple of months. Her boyfriend is catching the train tonight, so she figures she might as well go too.

She calls her Master for permission, but he doesn't answer. She leaves a message:

"Master Kisen, may I have permission to go home this weekend? I'd like to see my family."

Turning back to Akim, she sighs. "I hope he calls back. I know I waited till the last minute."

"I'm sorry, babe. I just found out," Akim says.

"I know. It's not your fault."

Her phone rings.

"Hello, Hope. Yes, you can go home. You're doing really well; wish your little sister were more like you." Master Kisen hangs up.

Hope lowers her phone. "Wow. I wonder what that was about."

"What's wrong?" Akim asks.

"Oh, nothing. I just feel better talking to Master Kisen than his father. That man is mean, scary. If Kisen wasn't in charge, I wouldn't have called. I wonder what my little sister has been up to now."

She finishes packing and calls her father to pick her up at the train station. She mentions what Kisen said about Destinee. Now she knows something's going on. Gabriel tells her what's happened with her sister, but reassures her not to worry. "She'll be home Sunday. Maybe you can talk some sense into her before it's too late."

"Come on, Hope, we've got a train to catch," Akim interrupts.

The station is only two blocks from campus. As they approach, they see drones circling and hear sirens; the Retrievers, coming for slaves trying to escape.

Hope looks at Akim. "Why do they keep trying? Don't they know it's impossible with these chips?"

The Retrievers rush past them toward a couple convulsing on the sidewalk, their chips activated. It's not an unusual sight, especially near the train station. Slaves try hiding under train cars, thinking they can endure the pain until the train gets farther from the towers where the chips won't register.

The station is crowded. It's the weekend, so many students are allowed to visit family. The train is also the main transportation for slaves, unless they hold high-level jobs and can afford a car. Hope's family has two vehicles, one for her father and one for her mother. Akim could afford one from the sale of his paintings, but he saves his money toward buying their freedom instead.

After a two-hour ride, Hope reaches her stop. Akim has another hour to go. He kisses her goodbye as she departs. Gabriel is waiting when she exits the train. On the way home, they talk about Destinee. They'll have to straighten her out before it's too late.

Hope walks into a dark house. Her little brothers are hiding, ready to scare her like always. She plays along, bracing for the attack.

"BOO!" they shout, jumping on her. They all tumble to the floor, wrestling and laughing. Everyone is happy to see Hope. They wish Destinee were there too, just a couple more days.

Chapter 8
A Lesson for Destinee

———

Destinee is awakened by the alarm blaring. Mercy is already up getting dressed. The door suddenly bursts open and the attendant throws Destinee's clothes on her bed.

"Don't bother putting your uniform on; you're going home."

"I'm going home?"

"Yes. Say your goodbyes. I'll be back in about fifteen minutes."

Destinee looks at Mercy, who sits on the bed trying to hide her tears. Destinee sits beside her and puts her arms around her.

"I'm sorry, Destinee. I wish you were staying longer."

"It's okay. I know I'm a mess." They laugh and hug.

"Destinee, you need to get your act together or you'll end up back here with me. I'm not your personal bodyguard; you'll have to pay me." Mercy laughs, then the tears come again.

"Why am I crying? I've only known you two damn days."

"Don't cry. I promise I'll visit; you're my best friend. Meeting you is the best part of coming here."

"I'm glad we met too. Promise me you'll be good."

"I promise."

"Now hurry up and get dressed before they change their minds."

The attendant opens the door. "Come on, girl; let's go." Destinee gives Mercy another hug and rushes out to the headmaster's office, wondering whether her parents will be angry or so overjoyed they forget to be mad. When she reaches the office there's no sign of her parents; the headmaster's door is closed. The secretary tells her to take a seat. Destinee is overjoyed, waiting to see who came for her.

The door opens. Destinee jumps up to embrace them, but it's Master Kisen.

"Don't look so disappointed. Be happy I didn't leave your ass here."

"I am happy, thank you, sir. I just expected my parents."

"They couldn't pick you up. I brought you, so I'm the one who can take you out."

Destinee climbs into the back seat. Master Kisen watches her in the rearview mirror and notices the bruises on her face.

"What happened to you?"

"I got jumped, sir."

"Well, you do like to fight," he laughs.

"Did you win?"

"No sir. It was five of them."

She notices he isn't heading toward her house. She's not allowed to ask questions, so she waits. He stops in a part of the city she's never seen, in front of an apartment building. He hesitates, then tells her to come along. He buzzes them in with a card. At the front desk a very beautiful white woman smiles at Master Kisen but doesn't acknowledge Destinee; something she's used to; whites often look past slaves unless they need something from them.

They take the elevator to the third floor and walk to room 33. Master Kisen opens the door and tells Destinee to go in. She sees a bed and feels a fresh wave of fear; she's heard of Masters raping their slaves when they reach a certain age, and she's about that age. Tears well, but she keeps her head down. He tells her to shower; she goes without looking at him, crying under the water.

He knocks and tells her to open the door. She wraps a towel around herself and opens it. He hands her a bag. "Put these on." She closes the door and opens the bag, a new set of clothes. "You can't go home in dirty clothes, can you?"

Destinee smiles and changes, relieved and happy. She fixes her hair and brushes her teeth; there's even a little bottle of cologne in the bag. She's never worn cologne before. She walks out with a big smile, and

24

Master Kisen coughs. "Girl, you overdid it with the cologne; you were only supposed to put a little on. Smells like the whole bottle." She laughs, but he's still coughing.

"Come here, Destinee. Sit down, we need to talk."

She sits at the foot of the bed. He pulls up a chair, takes her hands, and meets her eyes.

"Look at me. You were afraid, weren't you?"

"Yes sir."

"I showed you two paths: stay on this one, complete your studies, go to college like your sister, or go back to reform school until you're of age and end up in a room with a man doing whatever he wants. You're a smart girl, Destinee. Make your parents proud. They worked to put you at a level most slaves don't reach. Be grateful for what they did, and for what I've done. If my father were handling this, he'd have left your ass in reform school until you were eighteen. He wouldn't be wasting his time on you. So get your shit together, and let's go home."

"Master Kisen, I've learned my lesson. I'm not the same person I was two days ago. You'll see, and thank you for another chance."

"Don't tell me; show me. This will be your last chance."

Chapter 9
Lesson Learned

———

The front door suddenly opened, and Destinee ran in with Master Kisen walking behind her. She yelled for her mom and dad, but Hope appeared at the top of the stairs and rushed down with her little brothers close behind. Their parents came in from the kitchen.

Everyone gathered in the living room, hugging Destinee and welcoming her home. Jesse noticed her bruised face.

"What happened to you?"

"I got jumped."

"And you lost? She must've been bigger than you," asked Samuel.

"The odds were five to one."

"That's not fair," replied Seth.

"Life's not fair," she said.

Then Destinee did something that shocked everyone; she walked over to Master Kisen, wrapped her arms around him, and hugged him. Looking up at him, she said, "Thank you for everything you've done for me."

Stunned, he patted her on the back. "Remember what I told you."

"I will, sir."

Everyone froze. Master Kisen himself was surprised; he had never interacted with a slave like that before, and being touched by one was a major taboo. Destinee's parents were terrified; you do not touch a white person, especially your Master. But instead of getting angry, Kisen had awkwardly, almost reluctantly, hugged her back. The moment ended quickly, but the fear in her parents didn't. They had witnessed something that normally would mean severe punishment.

Destinee ran upstairs, her brothers following. Gabriel, still shaken, turned to Kisen. "Sir, I'm so sorry. Please forgive her."

"Forgive her for what?" Kisen chuckled. "She's not a bad girl."

"I know, sir. We've talked to her about fighting so many times. I think she gets picked on because she's got it better than most. We'll let Hope talk to her."

"That's why I brought her home early; so she'd have time with her sister."

Jesse stepped forward. "Thank you, sir, for being understanding."

Kisen nodded. "Your daughter has seen things that should scare her straight. That was the idea. I hope it works."

He turned to leave. "Enjoy your weekend." He glanced at Hope and smiled before walking out the door.

As soon as he was gone, everyone went to Destinee's room.

"What is wrong with you? Have you lost your mind? You don't touch a white person, especially Master. You could've ended up back at reform school!"

"You saw he didn't mind. I'm grateful for what he's done. Taking me there was the best thing he could've done for me. Mom, I'm not the same person I was; I'm better."

Destinee told her family about the reform school, her new friend Mercy who looked out for her, and her talk with Master Kisen afterward. She explained that she now realized how lucky she was and wouldn't let them, or Kisen, down. Then she told them about Mercy's story: how she'd been there since she was nine, with no family, no visitors, no one.

"Mom, Mercy has no one. She's all alone. She's my friend, my best friend."

"How is she your best friend? You've only known her two days," her father said.

"In those two days we bonded. She took care of me, made me see how lucky I am to have family. She wishes she had what I have. If she did, she wouldn't be there. I owe my life to her, and to Master Kisen."

"If she was watching out for you, how'd you get jumped?" Jesse asked.

"That was my fault. She told me not to leave the room without her, but I did."

"Hard-headed ass," Jesse smirked.

Chapter 10
Hope has a visitor

Sunday morning, Hope was awakened by Destinee jumping on her bed.

"Get up, get up, spend some time with me before you go back to school."

"Oh my… at least let me open my eyes."

"Okay, I'll stay right here till you do."

"Why did you hug your Master?"

"My Master? He's your Master too."

"I don't like calling him that."

"You didn't mind before you went to your precious university," Destinee laughed.

"When you see what's out there, in countries that are free, it changes you. I've changed, Sweetie. Didn't reform school change you too?"

"Yes."

"Then we've both changed, for the better. Remember that."

The sisters got dressed and went downstairs for breakfast.

"What time is your train?" Gabriel asked.

"It leaves at three."

"Master Kisen is on his way. He wants to see you before you go."

"Why?"

"I don't know. He didn't say."

Jesse stood in front of Hope, taking her hand. "Are you sure you don't know? Is everything alright at school?"

"Mother, everything is fine."

"I guess we'll find out when he gets here," Destinee shouted from upstairs.

Hope was nervous but hid it from her parents. She had no idea what Master Kisen wanted. She worried the school might have contacted him; she'd been outspoken about slavery and involved in cliques that had already landed her in trouble, with threats of contacting her Master. But she was close to graduation and had pulled back from those groups. She prayed that wasn't the reason.

The mood in the house grew heavy. When a Master asked to see you, it was usually bad news. And this Master was still new; they hardly knew him. He'd only been there twice before: once to introduce himself when he took over the family business after his father's illness, and again when he brought Destinee home.

The doorbell rang. Gabriel opened it. "Come in, sir."

Master Kisen stepped inside, glanced at Hope. "I want to talk to you. Let's step outside."

Hope looked at her parents, then followed him out.

"The school contacted me," he began. She stiffened, thinking she was in trouble. Instead, he said, "I received your grades. I'm proud of you. You're going to be a great doctor."

She couldn't believe it. She wanted to look at him, but kept her head down. This was the first time he had ever spoken to her directly. She remembered seeing him as a boy around the plantation, until Master Brown had sent him away. She whispered, "Thank you."

"I'm going to find you a hospital to work in, and an apartment."

"That's not necessary, sir. I plan to live with my parents. My boyfriend and I decided it's the best way to save money to buy our freedom."

Kisen couldn't stop staring. She was the most beautiful woman he had ever seen, black or white. Smart too. A doctor. He thought he could stand there all day.

"You can go in. Send your father out."

"Yes, sir. And thank you."

Gabriel came outside, worry on his face.

"Don't worry," Kisen said. "Nothing's wrong. I just told her how proud I am. She's graduating at the top of her class. You must be proud. You've done well with your kids. We'll get Destinee straight too."

"Yes, sir. That scare tactic you used should help."

"Go on, spend time with your family."

As Kisen walked to his car, Destinee ran out.

"Master Kisen!" She grabbed his hand. He knew it broke every rule of etiquette, but he let her, smiling down at her. She looked like her big sister, just smaller.

"Make me proud," he said.

"I will, sir. I promise."

The whole family watched from the doorway. Gabriel turned to Jesse. "You need to talk to your daughter about proper etiquette before she ends up back at reform school."

"I will. But one thing's for sure, he's nothing like his father."

"No, he's not. Master Brown was never friendly to his slaves. If it were up to him, we'd still be living in shacks on the plantation, with him taking everything we earned. This one... he's different."

Chapter 11
Old Master Brown

Master Brown, Kisen's father, was in the early stages of dementia. Because of this, his business had to be managed by his three children. A gathering was held on the plantation to divide the slaves among them. The slaves also learned which of Master Brown's children they would be left to in his will.

Master Brown was old school. He despised the new laws dictating how slaves should be treated. To him, they were his property, and no one had the right to tell him what to do with his own. He hated the idea of them keeping part of their earnings; he wanted it all. As for the new rules on punishment, he dismissed them entirely. He believed in the old-fashioned way.

The family businesses were now run by Kisen, while his brother and sister managed plantation matters, aside from the slaves, except their own. The Browns were already beyond wealthy, and with the constant flow of income from their slaves, they were among the richest families in the United States.

The slaves preferred being under Master Kisen's authority. He was fair and treated them with respect. The youngest son, Cruse, was cruel, mean since childhood, and they dreaded the thought of falling under his care. Their sister, Kiya, treated them strictly as slaves. Spoiled by her father, she never lifted a finger herself. If you were assigned to her, you worked hard.

Gabriel knew his family was better off with Kisen. On the plantation, he often came to the aid of slaves mistreated by Cruse. Once Kisen assumed responsibility for them, he rarely interfered unless absolutely necessary. They knew their duties, and he left them to it. He preferred running the family companies to acting as a slave owner anyway.

Driving back to the plantation one evening, Kisen couldn't get Hope out of his mind. Her beauty was unlike anything he'd ever seen. He tried to focus on work, but his thoughts kept drifting back to her. As he passed his father's house, he saw him sitting on the porch. Kisen honked and waved, but Master Brown motioned for him to stop.

Kisen backed up his truck and walked onto the porch.

"What is it, Dad?"

"Where you been all day? You know we got work to do around here."

"Dad, you don't have anything to do. Just rest."

"Damnit, boy, I been resting all day. I'm tired of resting. Take me to my office."

"Come on, Dad." Kisen helped him inside the dimly lit house. "Damn, Dad, turn some lights on."

"Why should I? That's what slaves are for. Louis! Get in here and turn on this light."

"The switch is right here. I'll get it."

Louis rushed in. "Yes sir, what do you need?"

"Never mind, Louis. I got it," Kisen said, shaking his head at his father.

He guided him into the office. "What do you need in here?"

"Need to take a count of my slaves. I think some are missing."

"Dad, none of your slaves are missing. Come on, let's get you ready for bed."

"Where's your mother? Tell her to come in here."

"Dad… Mom's gone."

"Gone where?"

"Mom died five years ago."

Kisen sat silently, watching tears roll down his father's face. He wished he had spent more time with him, gotten to know him better. Maybe his mother's death had hardened him, made him withdraw into work, neglecting his children. Kisen loved him, but his father had always been stern, too busy building his empire to be a father. And now look at him.

Kisen had never understood why his father treated slaves so badly, nor why Cruse followed his example. His father always said, "You have to put fear in them. Make them afraid to cross you, or they'll try you." Kisen never agreed. He believed respect earned respect. He had little direct experience managing slaves, but he had already decided he would never be like his father.

"Well, Dad, I have to get home. I've got paperwork to do."

Kisen led him to bed and tucked him in.

"I'll stop by in the morning, Dad."

Kisen finally reached his house, set back from his father's and siblings'. He liked the seclusion, away from everyone. The difference showed even in the number of slaves, just a minimal few to keep the household running. Nothing like his brother's and sister's houses near their father's estate, where slaves hovered around them constantly: opening doors as if they couldn't do it themselves, running their bathwater, drying them off, rubbing lotion on their bodies, manicuring nails, combing hair, dressing them, all before they even stepped out of their bedrooms.

That was exactly how his father had run his home before falling ill. Now, only the essentials remained. Kisen, though, had always been different. He didn't need pampering, thought it ridiculous to be so helpless. He kept only enough slaves to handle the basics, cooking, cleaning, a chauffeur, and pilots for his planes and helicopters.

As he reached for the door, it opened. His butler, who also managed the house, took his jacket. Though a slave, Kisen considered him a trusted friend.

"Shall I have the cook prepare you something, sir?"

"No, I'm good," Kisen replied.

He went to his study, trying to bury himself in work and get Hope out of his head, but it didn't help. Opening his laptop, he pulled up the registry of his slaves and searched for Hope's name.

Her record was impressive: straight-A student, talented, played piano, sang, loved the arts. She was valuable, and soon to be a doctor.

He smiled and closed the laptop.

Chapter 12
Hopes Plans

Gabriel called for Hope. "Come on, Hope, before you miss the train."

Hope ran down and hopped in the car. "Where's Destinee?"

"She's staying. We need to talk."

Jesse turned around and looked at Hope. "Has Master Kisen decided what hospital you'll be working at?"

"Yes. We talked about it. I'm going to work at your hospital and live at home with my family," she replied with a smile.

"I plan on living at home and saving my money to buy..." Hope stopped abruptly.

Gabriel noticed her hesitation. "Buy what?"

"Oh, nothing, Dad."

"What were you about to say, Hope? What are you hiding?"

"Nothing, Daddy."

"Girl, you think I don't know when you're hiding something? Go ahead, spill it."

"Akim and I are saving money to buy our freedom and move to Paris."

"It doesn't matter how much money you save. Master Kisen and Akim's master won't let you go. You're both too valuable; you're going to be doctors. You can give up that idea."

"Akim has already started saving money from selling his paintings. We're planning to purchase our freedom through the Underground. We're not going to live our lives as slaves when there's freedom everywhere else. You should do the same. Haven't you heard of the

Underground, Dad? They have a secret club on campus. I've attended some meetings and met members. They do exist, and that's how I'm going to purchase my freedom."

"You'd better stay away from those organizations, especially at school. You know they're being watched."

Gabriel came to a sudden stop. Flashing blue lights filled the street. A group of slaves lay on the ground, their punishment chips activated. He looked at Hope in the rearview mirror. "How do you plan on escaping with these chips? You won't get far."

"The Underground has helped thousands escape. Whatever they're doing works, and it'll work for me, Daddy."

Gabriel pulled up at the train station. Hope hugged her mom, then her dad. Gabriel whispered in her ear, "Don't worry, sweetheart. I promise you'll get your freedom, one day soon. Now go to school."

Jesse looked at Gabriel. "I heard you. How can you make a promise like that?"

Gabriel smiled.

"Like you told Hope, you think I don't know when you're hiding something."

"I'm not hiding anything, Jesse. I'll tell you everything when the time is right."

"It's the Underground, isn't it?"

"See, Jesse? Don't talk about the Underground. Stay quiet and don't ask questions."

"Why?"

"When the time is right, I'll tell you everything. You might be needed."

Chapter 13
Gabriel sees the light

———❧———

Gabriel walks into his office and finds James waiting.

"Good morning, Gabriel. Just wanted to let you know we have another meeting tonight. Can you make it?"

"Yes, I'll be there," replies Gabriel.

James tells him he'll get him caught up on what the organization has accomplished and what's planned for the near future. He glances around the office.

"Come on, let's step outside."

As they walk out, James studies him. "What's wrong? Did something happen over the weekend?"

Gabriel explains the conversation with his daughter, her plans to purchase her freedom through the Underground and move to Paris. "I know it won't happen anytime soon, but I want my family to stay together. If she leaves, I might never see her again."

"Did you tell her you're a member of the Underground?"

"No. I remember what you said, no one is to know."

James smiles. "Good. But I'm sure you and your wife have enough saved to buy your freedom and go with her."

Gabriel then tells him about Destinee's weekend in reform school for fighting, and how much worse it could have been under their previous master, Master Brown. Luckily, his son is more understanding.

"If everything falls into place, you won't have to worry. Your family will stay together, and free."

"How long are we looking at, James? One year, five, ten, twenty?"

"Gabriel, we're planning to accomplish this within a year, two at most if things don't go as planned with the election."

"I hope you're right. I never thought about freedom until I spoke with my daughter. We have a good life, at the top of our class."

"Yes, Gabriel, you have a good life for a slave. But don't you want more for your family? Your daughter does. And what about the slaves who don't have your advantages? The ones at the bottom, without opportunity or education, what about them?"

James pats him on the back. "Meet at my place at 8:00."

Chapter 14
Passing of Seth

———✦———

Samuel and Seth are having a normal day at school, but Seth hasn't been feeling well this morning. He raises his hand. "May I go to the restroom? I'm not feeling well."

The teacher excuses him. He slowly gets up, but before he reaches the door he collapses to the floor. Samuel runs to him. "Seth? Seth, what's wrong?"

The teacher sprints down the hall to fetch the nurse. By the time the nurse arrives, Seth is unconscious. The nurse calls the EMTs. The principal calls Master Kisen and Jesse to explain what happened and that he's on his way to the hospital, the same hospital where Jesse works. Jesse calls Gabriel and tells him she's on her way.

Jesse arrives at the emergency room just as the ambulance pulls in. Seth is rushed inside; Gabriel and Jesse are led to see him. Blood is coming from his mouth, nose, and ears. Jesse has seen this before; she knows what's happened. She looks at Gabriel, eyes full of tears. "This is my fault. I did this." She turns and runs from the room. Gabriel follows. "What do you mean, this is your fault?"

"It's those damn chips, Gabriel." She's frantic. "I told them the chips needed to be removed by age six. Keeping them in past that is unsafe, but they wouldn't listen; they were looking at cost. Thousands of kids have died because of those chips. Now I'm losing my baby to something I helped create."

"Babe, it's not your fault. You can't blame yourself."

She rushes back to her son's room and tells the doctor, "Take him to the operating room. You have to remove the chips, that's what's killing him. Please, take them out before it's too late."

Master Kisen arrives as they are rushing Seth to emergency surgery. Gabriel tells him what happened and what Jesse said about the chips. They sit in the waiting room, waiting for Jesse. She returns in tears. "I don't think he's going to make it. It's too late."

Gabriel holds Jesse and they cry. Master Kisen sits across from them, feeling the weight of their grief. This is not the detached pity of a man who's lost property; he feels something deeper. He can't help it; he feels their pain.

A doctor approaches Gabriel and Jesse. He has known Jesse for years, having worked with her when the chips were implanted. He takes Jesse's hand. "I'm so sorry, Jesse. I did everything I could, but it wasn't enough."

Gabriel and Jesse stand in the waiting room, holding each other and crying. Master Kisen crosses to them and wraps his arms around them. He's moved to tears; they welcome the embrace despite everything.

Master Kisen tells them to go home, he'll take care of everything. He leaves and walks down the hall while the hospital staff, composed of slaves and freemen, watch him pass. They're stunned; they have never seen a Master show compassion like this.

Kisen is legally responsible for Seth since the boy is his property. He's seen his father dispose of slaves before, cremation was always the cheapest method, but he won't discard this little boy that way.

Gabriel and Jesse know how slaves are put away: cremated or buried in the slave cemetery with a cross that lists name, birth date, and death date. This will be the last time they see their son's face. Now they must tell Samuel, Destinee, and Hope that their brother is gone. Jesse kisses Seth on the cheek. "Goodbye, my beautiful baby. Till we meet again."

Master Kisen sits in the hospital administrator's office to make arrangements. While waiting he wonders why he's feeling this way about his slaves. He's never seen his father or siblings show such feeling. Their father treated slaves like commodities, mentally and physically abusive, willing to send them to clinics as research subjects or organ donors if they weren't valuable. Cruse, his brother, took after their father but treated slaves as amusement, favoring low-class slaves so punishment would be less severe. His sister was lazy and spoiled, surrounding herself with the most attractive slaves because their looks amused their father.

Growing up watching his family treat slaves that way made Kisen sick. His father always said, "You have to make them fear you." Kisen never agreed, yet now he is responsible for the same slaves. He remembers his father saying he was too soft to handle slaves; so why was he put in charge?

The administrator breaks his reverie. "Sir, are you ready to claim the body?"

"Yes," Kisen replies.

"Would you like me to make arrangements for selling the organs?" the administrator asks.

"Hell no. Leave his organs alone. I will claim his body whole."

Chapter 15
Master Keisens Gift

Gabriel calls Hope on their way home and tells her she needs to make arrangements to come back; it's a family emergency. They can't tell her why; they'll explain when she arrives.

When Gabriel and Jesse pull into the driveway, Destinee and Samuel run to the car, peering into the backseat for their brother.

"Where is he? Does he have to stay in the hospital?" Samuel asks.

Jesse begins to cry uncontrollably.

"Mom, why are you crying? Where's Seth?"

Gabriel helps Jesse out of the car, and they all go inside. The children can tell from their mother's sobbing that their brother isn't coming home. The house is filled with crying the whole night.

Gabriel remembers the meeting he was supposed to have with James. He tells his wife he'll be back, that he needs fresh air. As he steps outside, the rain begins. Instead of driving, he walks, then runs, faster and faster. The harder he runs, the harder it rains, thunder and lightning cracking overhead. It feels like God is speaking to him. He falls to his knees and looks up at the sky.

"What are you trying to tell me?" he whispers.

The rain mixes with his tears, which turn into anger. Suddenly he hears sirens and sees blue lights. He realizes it's past curfew and he's running in the streets. He stands still, waiting for the police.

"What are you doing out here after curfew, and where are you going?"

"I'm sorry, sir. I didn't realize the time. My son died today, and I just needed to walk."

"Who's your Master?" asks one of the officers, both of them free blacks.

They notice Gabriel's black clothing, marking him as a class 5 slave. His chip hasn't triggered either, so escape seems unlikely.

"I guess you're not trying to run, being one of those high-class slaves. Roll up your sleeve, let me take a look."

Gabriel does as told.

"Take your ass home. And I'm sorry about your son."

The officers get back in their car and drive off. Gabriel, already on James Street, decides to keep going. By the time he reaches James's house, he's drenched, his tears hidden by rain.

The meeting is already underway, so James leads him to the basement. Gabriel apologizes for being late, then tells the group about his son's death.

"James, we have to get this done before any more of our children die, like my son."

"How many more are going to die before we get Anthony in the White House?" one member yells.

Another adds, "We outnumber them; why can't we just take over, go to war?"

James speaks softly over the uproar. "You all know why. Until we find where the chips are controlled, we can't do anything. The election is the way, the best way, the right way, the safe way. We don't want to lose any of our people."

He looks around the room. "The election is only two months away. People are working hard on this campaign. We've got this. You have to believe all our work isn't in vain. I believe."

Gabriel wipes his tears. "What if he doesn't get elected? What if we fail?"

"If he doesn't, we have a backup plan. There's always a backup plan. But Anthony will be our next President," James says with a smile.

"The whites are going to put him in the White House for us. If they only knew they were voting for a black man, they'd lose their minds."

Laughter breaks the tension. Even Gabriel cracks a smile. "Now go home and be with your family, Gabriel. They need you."

Gabriel turns to leave but remembers curfew and the police warning.

"Can someone give me a ride home? I'm not free like you all; I have a curfew."

When Gabriel returns home, he sits on the couch, staring upstairs at his son's room. Wishing it were all a bad dream, he walks up and pushes open the empty door. Samuel isn't in his bed. Jesse comes up behind Gabriel, wraps her arms around him, and rests her head on his shoulder.

"Samuel's in our bed. He couldn't sleep in there without his brother."

Chapter 16
The Funeral

———∿∿∿———

They walk into the room and lie on Seth's bed. Jesse picks up his pillow and holds it to her face.

"I can smell him, Gabriel."

She presses the pillow to Gabriel's face, and they both begin to cry.

Jesse whispers in Gabriel's ear, "I killed my son."

"Stop saying that, Jesse. You didn't put this chip in Seth."

"No, but these are my chips. I helped create these damn things."

"Yes, but you've been warning them how dangerous they are for kids, and they wouldn't listen. This isn't your fault."

"It's not that they wouldn't listen; they don't care. I'm being punished, babe, punished for all the kids who died because of me. This is God's punishment."

"Baby, you're doing what you had to do. You're a slave, not a free woman with a choice. None of us have a choice. We do what we're told, and you were told to do this. If anyone should be punished, it's them."

Gabriel and Jesse hear the front door open; it's Hope. They go downstairs.

"What is this family emergency I had to come home for?" she asks.

Jesse begins to cry again. "Sit down, sweetie."

"What's wrong, Mom?"

Gabriel and Jesse sit on either side of Hope and tell her what happened to Seth. She runs upstairs to his room, finds his bed empty, throws herself on it, and cries. Gabriel and Jesse sit beside her and cry with her.

When Hope finally falls asleep, Gabriel and Jesse check on Destinee, who is still asleep. Then they go to their room and lie beside Samuel, knowing he'll have the hardest time; he's lost his twin, the brother who's been by his side since birth.

The night is short; no one sleeps. Crying fills the house. Gabriel is awakened by the phone. It's Master Kisen.

"Yes, sir?"

"Good morning, Gabriel. I'm calling to let you know the arrangements have been made. It's a little different than usual."

"Different, sir?"

"Yes. We're going to have a funeral for Seth."

"A funeral, sir?"

"The funeral will be the day after tomorrow at 1:00 at the church. I've contacted everyone on our plantation. If there's anyone from outside, tell me and I'll contact their Masters so they can attend."

"Yes, sir. Thank you, sir."

Gabriel wakes his family and tells them what Master Kisen arranged. They're stunned, slaves don't have funerals; only white people or free blacks do.

"He's doing this for Seth?" Jesse asks.

"Yes. He said it would be different this time. He didn't have him cremated. We're going to see him, we're going to see our son. He's letting the plantation off to attend; all our family will get to say goodbye."

Jesse can't believe what Master Kisen is doing, but she's grateful; she's never been to a funeral. She calls her family and Gabriel's to tell them about the service and that Kisen has let them attend. Everyone is saddened by the accident and amazed at the Master's kindness. They've never seen anything like this from Old Master Brown or heard of any Master doing this for slaves.

Kisen knows his father will be angry, but it's his decision; his father will have to accept it; after all, he put Kisen in charge.

Still, there's no time to dwell on what his father might say; duty calls, and the morning's work awaits.

Kisen goes to the church early to open the gate for slaves who live off the plantation. The church sits behind the slave quarters. He enters and approaches the coffin, slowly opens it, and sees Seth, appearing to be sleeping. The mortuary did a good job. He leaves the casket open for the viewing.

The pastor arrives early to check things over.

"Hello, Pastor."

"Hello, Master Kisen. Is there anything I can do for you, sir?"

"No, just looking things over."

"Sir, this is a good thing you're doing for this family. Your father never allowed us a real funeral before. We never asked; actually, I don't think we've ever asked your father for anything," the Pastor says with a smile.

"I know. My father isn't happy, but this is something I wanted to do. Things may be changing around here."

"God bless you, sir."

Gabriel's family is the first to arrive, escorted by the Pastor.

They approach the casket and look down at Seth. "He looks like he's sleeping," Samuel says as he touches Seth's hand and begins to cry. Jesse kisses Seth's cheek. "Baby, I'm sorry." She notices the flowers and says, "The flowers are so beautiful."

"Master Kisen did all this?" she asks the Pastor.

"Yes, he did. I've never seen anything like this on the plantation. Master Kisen is indeed a good man."

People begin to file into the church, family and the curious; many have never attended a funeral. The church fills to capacity; some stand along the walls or outside. The Pastor opens the service with a choir song. Master Kisen slips in and stands at the back, trying not to be noticed, but how could he be? He's the only white person in the church.

Kisen enjoys the preaching and the singing. He usually sits on his porch and listens, but this is the first time he's witnessed it. He planned to leave early but can't pull himself away; this gospel music is nothing like the Catholic services he attends.

Suddenly the back doors burst open. "What the hell is going on in here?" shouts Old Master Brown, followed by his son Cruse. Everyone stares forward, afraid to look back.

"What the hell are you niggers doing? Get the hell back to work before I lock you in here and burn this damn church down."

Kisen stands and walks over to his father. "Dad, come on. Let's go."

"I'm not going anywhere; these are my niggers."

"Cruse, why did you bring him?"

"He wanted to come. You had no business doing this; slaves don't have funerals. This isn't right."

"Take him home. I'll be up when this is over."

Cruse takes his father by the arm and leads him away. Kisen returns to the front and tells the Pastor to continue. The Pastor directs the family to the casket to say their goodbyes. Jesse breaks down; Gabriel holds her up. Hope has her arms around Destinee and Samuel as they cling to her. People come up to view the body; it takes over an hour. Master Kisen is the last to step forward.

At the end of the service the Pastor praises Kisen for his kindness and closes the casket. The Pastor exits with the pallbearers carrying the casket, followed by the family and the rest of the congregation. Gabriel approaches Kisen.

"Sir, I know I'm not supposed to do this, but I have to say thank you. My family and I appreciate all you've done."

Destinee hugs him. "Thank you, sir."

Everyone is shocked; slaves don't touch their Masters. They expect Kisen to scold her, but instead he hugs her back. He hugs Hope, who keeps her arms at her sides, unsure what to do. He hugs Jesse, who also stands stiffly. Then he shakes hands with Samuel and Gabriel. Kisen's display of kindness shocks the plantation, but the Pastor smiles and thanks God for what he's witnessed.

Kisen walks with the family to the cemetery and stays until the burial is complete. On his way home he finds his father, brother, and sister on the porch and decides to get it over with.

"All right, let it out," he says.

Cruse snaps, "What the hell do you think you're doing, Kisen? Having a funeral for a slave; this isn't right."

"They lost their son. I wanted to do this for them."

Master Brown asks, "Why? They're just slaves. Plus, look at how much money you lost by letting them miss work."

"We're not hurting for money." Kisen looks at his sister. "Do you have anything to say?"

"No, big brother. I'm not in it; I'm just here."

"If you're done, I'm going home."

"Don't let this shit happen again, Kisen."

"Yes, Daddy."

Chapter 17
Getting Acquainted

The family's drive home was silent, no one said a word. You would occasionally hear a sniffle, but not a word. When they arrive home, everyone silently walks to their rooms, except for Hope, instead she lays on the couch. She's thinking about everything Master Kisen has done. She would love to call and thank him again. She begins to dial his number, but hangs up, she dials again.

"Hello Hope, is everything alright?"

"Yes sir, I just wanted to say thank you for what you did for my family, everything was beautiful,"

"You're welcome."

"Everyone is gone to their rooms; it's been an exhausting day."

"Well sir, I need to get my things together, I need to catch my train back to school tonight."

"Why, you just buried your brother, you can have more time off to spend with your family."

"Thank you, but I need to get back, I have to finish up my studies, and it's so hard being here."

"What time is your train?"

"It's at 7:00 sir."

"OK, you take care of yourself Hope."

"I will sir."

Hope hangs up the phone and goes upstairs to tell her parents she's sorry but has to go back to school. She then goes to her sister's room to say goodbye. She saves her little brother for last, knowing this will be the hardest. She opens his door slowly.

"Samuel, are you awake?"

Hope finds him lying on his brother's bed, staring at the ceiling. She knows this is going to be hard for him; Seth has been his constant companion since birth.

"I wish I could stay home with you, little brother, but I have to get back to school. If you need me, just call." She pauses. "I know this is hard for you, but remember, as long as you think about him, he still lives. He's watching over you."

She hugs and kisses him goodbye. "Try to get some sleep, Sweetie."

Hope opens her parents' door to see if her father can take her to the train station, but when she finds them asleep, she can't bring herself to wake them. She softly closes the door and calls a cab.

The ride to the train station is short, but Hope is consumed with memories of Seth, wishing she had spent more time with him and Samuel instead of being preoccupied with school, her grades, and her freedom. If she could do it over, she would have been a better sister.

Her thoughts are interrupted by the abrupt stop.

"Sorry about that. This is your stop," says the cab driver.

Hope steps out and notices someone standing by the gate. She wonders why a white man is standing at a gate posted for Blacks only. As she approaches, she realizes it's Master Kisen.

"Hello, Hope."

"Hello, Master Kisen. Is something wrong?"

"Come on, I'm giving you a ride back to school."

"Sir, that's a long drive."

"I don't have anything to do. I can't sleep anyway."

Hope opens the door and climbs into the back seat.

Master Kisen drives, talking to Hope through the rearview mirror, but he starts to get frustrated after almost running off the road.

"My God, I can't do this. I'll end up running into the back of a car or killing us both."

He pulls to the side of the road. "Come on, get up front."

Hope looks at him. "Sir, what did you say?"

"You heard me. Get in the front."

"But…"

"Hope, get your ass in the front."

Hope climbs into the front seat, nervous. She knows Blacks aren't supposed to ride in the front with whites, but he's her Master.

He looks at her and laughs. "You're alright. It's not against the law for you to sit in the front. Plus, you belong to me."

"Yes, sir."

He drives, trying to hold a conversation with Hope, but she answers with one-word responses.

"Hope, relax. Stop being so nervous. Talk to me."

Kisen keeps trying, and after a while Hope begins to relax, even smile. She tells him about college and her plans to live with her parents after graduating to save money.

He asks what she's saving for. She catches herself and smiles. "Nothing specific."

"The girl's going to be a doctor. We haven't had many doctors from the plantation; just you and your mother. I'm proud of you, Hope. I'm proud of your whole family."

"Thank you, sir."

Since neither of them has eaten, they were preoccupied with the funeral, Master Kisen suggests continuing their conversation over a meal. He drives around looking for a restaurant. They finally find one, but Hope hesitates; it's a white restaurant.

Kisen takes her by the hand and leads her in. Everyone in the restaurant stares as they sit in a booth. The waitress walks up to Master Kisen.

"Sir, I can serve you, but I can't serve her. This is an all-white restaurant. The Black restaurant is across the street."

He looks at the waitress, then across the street. "So how do I do this? I eat here and she eats across the street, even though she's my property?"

Before the waitress can respond, he grabs Hope by the hand. "Come on."

They walk across the street to the Black restaurant. The waitress seats them at a table. Service can be refused to a Black in a white restaurant, but not to a white in a Black one. The customers are all Black but avert their eyes out of respect for Master Kisen.

Master Kisen and Hope finally get to eat.

"This is better than the food across the street anyway," says Master Kisen with a smile.

They spend the night eating, talking, and laughing. The two-hour trip to the University flies by, and both are disappointed when it ends. Hope is so comfortable with Master Kisen she finds herself telling him her dream of visiting Paris one day. She even catches herself looking him in the eyes.

"Sir, I apologize for looking at you. I mean no disrespect."

"Hope, you have my permission to look at me all you want, as long as I can look at you," he says with a smile.

They arrive at Hope's dorm.

"I guess you'd better go in and get some sleep; I know you have your studies."

"Thank you, Master Kisen. Thank you for bringing me to school, and for what you did for my family today. You laid my brother away beautifully."

Hope begins to close the door.

"Hope, I wish you'd call me Kisen instead of Master Kisen."

"But I have to, sir."

"OK. You can call me Kisen when we're alone."

She leans her head in the window and whispers, "Good night, Kisen."

They both smile.

"Good night, Hope."

That night, they both think of each other. Hope doesn't know what to think of her Master. He's handsome, smart, funny, and kind, unlike any white or Black man she's ever met. She shakes her head in disbelief, wondering why she feels this way.

"Am I developing a crush on my Master, the man that owns me? Wow. This is crazy. I'm crazy."

She falls asleep with a smile, thinking about the night with her Master.

Master Kisen is experiencing the same thoughts while driving home. After she overcame her nervousness and saw him as a friend instead of her Master, she was comfortable enough to talk, laugh, and enjoy his company. He's wondering what it is about this woman that he can't get her off his mind.

Chapter 18
Destinee Request a Favor

The week had been quiet. Everyone slept in each morning since Master Kisen gave permission to take the rest of the week off and keep Samuel home. He felt they needed time to mourn, another act of unusual kindness from him.

As the week came to an end, no one paid attention to the outside world. They seldom left the house or even turned on the television. Whatever was happening elsewhere didn't matter; they were still hurting, especially Samuel, who missed Seth deeply.

Gabriel suddenly gets a call from James.

"I know it's a bad time, Gabriel, but I wanted to let you know, our man is in. He's on the ballot. We're almost there."

Gabriel hangs up, smiling for the first time since his son died. He goes upstairs to share the news with Jesse, but she doesn't receive it the same way. Her heart is broken, still heavy with grief. At the moment, she doesn't care about anything.

Gabriel looks in on Samuel and notices dinner still sitting untouched on the nightstand. Samuel is asleep in his brother's bed instead of his own.

"Samuel, you have to eat or you'll get sick."

"Dad, I don't care. I hurt too bad to eat."

"I know, son, I hurt too. But in time the pain will ease. You still have to eat."

"Yes, sir. Do I have to come downstairs?"

Gabriel kisses him on the forehead. "No, son. But you'll have to come out eventually. You have to go back to school."

He then makes his way to Destinee's room and knocks. "Come in."

"How are you feeling, sweetheart?"

"I'm fine, Dad. Just missing Seth."

"We all miss him. We always will."

"Dad, I need to talk to you about something."

"What is it?"

"Will you take me to the reform school to visit Mercy? I promised her I would. I miss her."

"I don't know about that, Destinee."

"Dad, she has no one. No one ever visits her. She took care of me, kept me safe from the other girls. I promised her."

"I'll have to talk to your mother and get Master Kisen's permission."

"Dad, I'll ask Master Kisen. We have a thing, you know." She smiles and winks.

He smiles back. "Yes, I've noticed you two have a thing, as you call it. But there's still your mother."

"Now's not a good time to ask her anything."

"I guess you're right."

Destinee doesn't waste time. She goes to her room, shuts the door, and thinks about what to say. She grabs a pad, writes it out, and when she's gathered enough courage, calls him.

"Master Kisen, this is Destinee. I'm calling to ask if I could go to the reform school to visit Mercy, please? Dad said I had to ask your permission."

"Who's Mercy?"

"She was my roommate at the reform school."

"Why do you need to visit her, Destinee?"

"She took care of me. She didn't let anything bad happen to me. She talked sense into me. I'm a better person because of her; she told me how lucky I was to have a family that cared, and a Master like you who taught me a lesson instead of leaving me there."

"You don't need to go back there."

"Please, sir. She has no family and a cruel Master who'll probably send her to a bordello like her mother in a few years."

Destinee tells Master Kisen the story of how Mercy ended up in reform school through no fault of her own, what happened to her family, and how she has no one. She reminds him she promised to visit her regularly.

Master Kisen, proud of Destinee for being so considerate, finally gives permission. "You promised, and you have to keep your word."

"Thank you so much, Master Kisen."

Destinee runs to tell her father. "He gave his permission. He'll call the reform school to let them know." Then she asks, "Can I go now?"

"Let me talk to your mother first."

Gabriel tries, but Jesse doesn't care. Right now, she doesn't care about much of anything.

Chapter 19
A Visit to Mercy

Mercy returned to her room from class. Suddenly, the intercom came on: *"Mercy, you have a visitor."*

She froze, bewildered; she'd never had a visitor before. Nervous and excited, she realized who it must be. *"It has to be Destinee. She promised she'd visit."*

Mercy entered the visitors' lounge and immediately spotted Destinee waiting at a table. She ran to her and hugged her; Destinee hugged back. They were both overjoyed.

"I told you I'd visit."

"I know, but I thought you'd forget about me once you walked out those doors."

"I could never forget you, lady."

They exchanged stories. Destinee told her about losing her brother Seth, and Mercy confessed she hadn't been the same since Destinee left. Sadness overcame her. She said she'd spent half her life in the facility and had three years left, but she didn't know what her Master planned. Would he give her a chance at college, or send her to a bordello like her mother, to a research facility, or make her an organ donor? He wasn't wealthy or smart, living only for the moment, doing what he could to make money now.

Mercy admitted she envied Destinee, wishing for a family like hers, a Master like hers, just someone to care. She knew if she had the chance, she'd soar.

She asked if Destinee had been staying out of trouble. Destinee smiled, saying yes, thanks to Mercy's advice, no fighting, good grades, and a clean record. She promised they'd be friends for life and that she'd visit every week, if Master Kisen allowed.

Their conversation was cut short by the blaring bell ending visiting hours. They hugged tightly. Destinee told her to keep her head up, that she'd be back.

Gabriel had been waiting in the car during the visit. Destinee got in, tears running down her face.

"Didn't you have a good visit?"

"Yes, sir. It was so nice to see her; she was happy to see me too. Do you know I'm the only visitor she's ever had?"

"I think meeting you showed her there's a better life than the one she was dealt."

"Daddy, I have an idea."

"What is it, sweetheart?"

"What if Mercy came to live with us?"

"Destinee, you know that's impossible. She has a Master. Do you have the money to buy her?" he chuckled.

"No, but you do. You and Mom make a lot of money."

"Yes, but a slave can't own a slave."

"Do you think Master Kisen would buy her?"

"Hell no. You and Master Kisen might have a thing, as you call it, but not that much of a thing. He wouldn't buy a slave just to make you happy, so don't even think about asking. You're getting too comfortable with your Master."

"If Master Kisen bought her, could she live with us?"

"Did you hear what I said, Destinee? Do you really think he'd do that just because you ask? And how do you know your mother would want another child to care for?"

"So if Mom said yes, it would be alright with you?"

"Why are we even talking about this? It's not going to happen. That would be a family decision. We just lost your brother, and now you want to bring someone else into the family?"

"Dad, I'll talk to Mom when the time is right."

"You'd need to talk to your brother and sister too."

"I will, but if everyone, including Master Kisen, said yes, would I have your permission?"

"If everyone said yes, it would be a miracle. But yes, you'd have my permission."

Gabriel pulled into the driveway. Before he even turned off the car, Destinee jumped out and ran inside. Jesse was in the kitchen cooking for the first time since Seth's death. Samuel had finally come out of his room and was sitting on the couch watching TV. Gabriel sat beside him, putting an arm around his son.

"Glad to see you out of your room."

Destinee came into the living room with her mom. "Sit down, Mom. I need to talk to you, Dad, and Samuel." She told them Mercy's story, about her parents, how she ended up at the Reform School, and how Destinee had cared for her there.

Jesse grew emotional. "Poor girl."

"Yes, Mom. She has no one. She's all alone except for me; we're sisters."

"What's going to happen to her?"

"I don't know. She has three more years in that horrible place."

Destinee then asked her parents if Master Kisen bought Mercy, could she live with them. She looked at Samuel.

"I don't care," he said quietly.

"Mom, I know it's a bad time…"

To Destinee's surprise, Jesse said yes. She looked at her father.

"I did say if you got a yes from everyone, I'd go along with it. But you still need your sister and Master Kisen. And I still don't think you should bring it to him."

"Daddy, please. What could he do? He likes me."

"Alright. You have my permission."

Destinee was overjoyed. She hugged everyone. "Thank you!"

"Don't forget, you need to call your sister first."

Destinee called her sister and explained about Mercy, asking if she'd be alright with her living with them if Master Kisen bought her.

"Why do you think Master Kisen would do this for you? It's not proper to ask him for favors. You're pushing it, little girl."

"He's a good man, a kind man, and he likes me."

Gabriel reminded Destinee to wait before asking Master Kisen. They were still grieving over Seth. It was too soon.

Chapter 20
Jesse Pleads her Case

This was Jesse's first day back at work since Seth died, and it felt overwhelming. There were more babies than usual, and she couldn't stop thinking about her son. Today she had to implant the very chips that killed him. With every implant she wondered if this one would malfunction and take another child's life. She asked to be relocated but was told no; there was nowhere else for her to go. So she continued, tears rolling down her face.

Loretta noticed her crying and pulled her aside.

"I don't want to implant these chips. They're killing these kids."

"Honey, the Board is looking into your concerns. They're finally listening. They want you to meet with the Board of Directors and bring your evidence."

"Baby, get back to work, knowing you're going to save these babies."

Jesse started crying again, tears of happiness and sadness, wishing she'd been given this chance sooner. She hugged Loretta. "Thank you."

"For what?"

"I know you did this."

"No, honey, it wasn't me. It was your Master."

"Master Kisen?"

"Yes. He met with the Board and told them they needed to listen to you about these chips. Lives have been lost, including your son's. Because of him they agreed to meet with you. The money his family donated to the hospital didn't hurt either."

"This man amazes me."

"Get your findings together and get it done."

"Oh my, I have to thank him."

"Girl, you have an awesome Master."

"When do we meet with them, Loretta?"

"I have no idea."

Jesse couldn't believe Master Kisen had arranged this for her. Suddenly her phone rang; it was him, calling to tell her to take the rest of the day off to prepare her documentation. The meeting would be at five o'clock. She thanked him and promised she'd be ready.

Master Kisen had to attend with her since she was a slave, and she knew it mattered because the Board was all white. But she felt hopeful. Her daughter had always said he was a good man, and she was beginning to see it herself, putting aside her belief that all white people were evil. Maybe she'd been wrong, maybe all but one were.

Jesse spent the day in her office gathering the materials for the meeting. At 4:30 she decided to go early to set up her PowerPoint. Master Kisen had said he'd meet her at 4:45, but she arrived first. The secretary showed her into the conference room. Anxiety hit hard. She'd never spoken to a room full of white people. Should she keep her head down to avoid eye contact? How could she present while staring at the floor?

Master Kisen walked in.

"Stop looking so nervous, Jesse. You can do this. Think about how long you've waited for this opportunity, and the kids you'll save."

"I first brought this to their attention five years ago."

"Then tell them that. And tell them how many children have died since. If you show them the financial loss from these deaths, they'll listen. I'm sorry, Jesse, but most slave owners don't care about the lives of their slaves unless they're making money off them. They're not making money from these kids yet, but the potential value they're losing will get their attention. That's all they care about: money."

"If you need to get angry because of Seth's death, then get angry.

What are they going to do? Nothing. You belong to me."

"You really care, don't you?"

"There are only a few like me, Jesse."

Board members began filing in, six men and five women, all white. No one acknowledged Jesse, but they all greeted Master Kisen and thanked him for coming. He spoke first and then introduced Jesse as a Class 5 Medical Doctor. They were impressed by her accomplishments, but congratulated him, not her; true enough, she wouldn't have achieved them without his support, but she was brilliant in her own right.

He told them she'd recently lost her child due to the chips remaining in children past their expiration point. Then he said, "From this point on, the floor is Jesse's." He reminded her not to be nervous; this was what she'd been waiting for: someone with the power to listen.

Jesse's presentation lasted an hour. She was very professional and didn't show her emotions; what would it accomplish? They didn't care about a slave's tears. When she finished, she thanked the Board for the opportunity and handed it over to Master Kisen, who also thanked them and said he'd wait for their decision.

They took the elevator down to the garage in silence. When they reached the car, Master Kisen said she'd done an amazing job and that he'd let her know the outcome.

She thanked him for arranging the chance to present.

He said he only wished it had come sooner before she lost her son.

Chapter 21
Hope has a Date

Hope is sitting in the library waiting for Akim. She tells him that Master Kisen has approved her working at the hospital where her mother is employed. She asks Akim if he asked his Master about working there too. She can see from his face it's not good.

"Akim, there's only a few more weeks till we graduate. We planned to work at the same hospital so we could see each other regularly. What did he say?"

"My Master said no. He wants me to work closer to home and open a studio for my paintings."

"What about our plans?"

"Our plans haven't changed. The studio is a good thing. The more paintings I sell, the closer we get to our goals."

"But when and how will we see each other? We're not from the same plantation."

"Our plans aren't going to change, Hope. I promise."

"How can you promise? We're at our Masters' mercy."

Hope grabs her books and walks out of the library. Akim runs after her.

"Hope, wait. Don't take this out on me. I'm trying."

"Akim, I know you're trying. I'm sorry. I have a lot on my mind, my brother, my family, graduation. I just need to be alone."

"I'll walk you to your dorm."

They walk in silence. When they reach her dorm, he kisses her on the forehead.

"Goodnight, baby."

"Goodnight, Akim."

Hope falls on her bed, staring at the moon through the skylight. She wonders how her future will play out. Will she and Akim really make it to Paris? Is she truly in love with him, or is it just their common goal, and his money, that binds them? Or will she live her life as a slave? She falls asleep with these thoughts swirling.

She's suddenly awakened by her phone ringing. She looks at it, expecting Akim's name, but it's Master Kisen. She feels nervous and excited at the same time.

"Hello, sir."

"Hey Hope, what are you doing?"

"Nothing, just overwhelmed with studying. Akim and I were in the library, and I needed a break."

"Come down, I'm parked out front."

"Yes, sir."

Hope rushes to the sink, washes up quickly, fixes her hair, powders her face, and changes her top. She's sick of the dull gray clothes she has to wear. Her roommate wakes up from the noise.

"You doing all this for Akim?"

She smiles. "No."

She runs downstairs, looking for Master Kisen's car, but it's nowhere in sight, only a shiny black truck with tinted windows. The window rolls down, and she hears Master Kisen's voice.

"Get in."

He laughs. "You can't climb in the back now, and the windows are tinted, so you don't have to worry about being seen."

She smiles and climbs into the truck, not noticing Akim approaching her dorm. He stands there watching the truck drive off. He can't see who's driving because of the tinted windows. He immediately dials her phone, but she left it on her bed in her haste.

Hope asks Master Kisen if something is wrong. He tells her no; he had such a good time bringing her to school that he wanted to see her again.

Hope smiles, realizing she had a good time too. She wants to ask where they're going but stops herself. No matter how comfortable she feels with him, he's still her Master, and she doesn't want to get too comfortable. Yet she's so at ease with him, and she knows he wouldn't mind. She sits quietly until he speaks.

"Now we're not going to do this again, are we?" Kisen asks.

"Tonight, I'm not your Master. We're friends, so relax."

"Yes, sir. Master Kisen."

He laughs. "What did I tell you to call me?"

"Sir, I can't. It would be disrespectful."

"I'm giving you permission to be disrespectful."

"Yes, sir… KISEN."

"That's better. Now what time is your class tomorrow?"

"I don't have any tomorrow."

"Good, you can stay out late."

They drive, talk, and laugh through the night. Kisen tells her about his trips around the world.

Hope loves hearing about the places he's been. She asks about Paris. "Did you go up the Eiffel Tower? Ride a boat down the Seine? What about the Louvre?"

"Slow down. Yes, I've done it all. That's your dream, to see Paris one day."

"It's just a dream."

"Dreams can come true, you know."

"Yes, dreams can come true for people like you, but not for people like me."

"Like you?"

"I'm sorry, I shouldn't have said that."

"Why not? Say what you feel. Remember, we're friends tonight. I'm not your Master."

"But you will be tomorrow, and you'll remember everything I said tonight. You know I can't say what I feel."

"What you say tonight disappears when the sun comes up, I promise. Now back to what you were saying, you don't think your dreams can come true?"

"No, sir."

"What do you dream of, Hope? Tell me."

"You promise what I say will disappear when the sun rises?"

"Yes, I promise," he says with a smile.

"I would love to one day live in Paris as a free woman."

She looks at him to see how he reacts to what she just said. To her surprise, he smiles.

"Remember what I said, dreams can come true. You never know what the future holds."

Then he reaches for her hand and kisses it. She's in disbelief, but she likes it.

It's getting late, but Hope is enjoying their time together and doesn't want the night to end. Kisen feels the same. He wonders if she's truly enjoying herself or just enduring it because she has no choice; he is her Master, so he asks,

"Are you enjoying yourself, Hope?"

"I am truly enjoying myself, Master Kisen; I mean, Kisen."

Kisen checks his watch and realizes the night has flown by.

"Hope, I didn't realize how late it is. We're closer to the plantation than the University. You can stay at the plantation, and I'll take you back in the morning."

Now she's nervous. She's heard stories of slaves being raped by their Masters. But Kisen doesn't seem like that. He's been so kind to her family, especially her brother. She realizes she's safe in his company, but still nervous.

They finally arrive at the plantation. The big black gate opens. They drive past the large plantation house where Master Brown lives, then Master Cruse's house, and then his sister Ms. Kiya's. Hope thinks if any of them saw her, they'd flip out. They reach Kisen's secluded house behind the trees. He pulls his truck into a garage filled with every vehicle imaginable. He loves his collection of cars. They sit there looking at each other for a moment.

He laughs. "Are you ready? Don't be nervous. I won't bite, unless you want me to."

She's still nervous as she slides out of the truck. Kisen puts his hand on her back and guides her inside. They're met by the butler, who's surprised to see Hope but quickly turns to Master Kisen.

"Sir, do you need anything?"

"No, James. Go to bed. I'm alright."

James tells them goodnight and leaves.

She recognizes the butler too; he attends church with her family.

She wonders if he'll say anything.

Kisen sees the concern on her face. "Don't worry. What goes on in my house stays in my house, even for my slaves."

Master Kisen leads her to the theater in the basement. She's never seen anything like it; a huge room with large couches covered in soft pillows, and a massive screen covering the wall.

"Your house is beautiful. I've passed your father's house my whole life and never seen the inside."

"Be glad you didn't."

"I know. Usually when slaves were called to your father's house, it wasn't good."

"You're right about that."

"I never thought I'd see the inside of any plantation house. I never expected it to look so magnificent."

"Thank you. What's your preference, western, comedy, drama, romance, or horror?"

"It doesn't matter. I'll probably fall asleep halfway through."

"OK, I'll pick. Horror, so you can hold on to me." He laughs.

Kisen invites Hope to sit down and make herself comfortable while he fixes them a drink. She walks around the room, admiring everything, the fabrics of silk and velvet, the paintings of movie stars.

"This is how they live, in the luxury we work for."

She doesn't know how to feel, anger or envy, all she knows is she feels overwhelmed by what she's experiencing.

Kisen returns with drinks. They spend the night watching the movie, with Hope jumping at every scare, grabbing onto Kisen. He laughs and pulls her close.

"I'll protect you."

They both get caught up in the moment, forgetting the movie. Hope falls asleep in his arms until she's awakened by a kiss on the forehead. She looks up at him. He kisses her softly on the lips.

"Do you want me to stop?" he asks.

"No," she whispers.

He kisses her again, then turns off the television. They lay in the darkness in each other's arms until they fall asleep.

Morning arrives. Kisen wakes, lying there watching the beautiful Black woman sleeping in his arms. He's experiencing feelings he's never felt before.

He hears the door open and looks up. It's the butler.

"Sir, I'm sorry to disturb you. I noticed you weren't in your room, just checking to see if you needed anything?"

"No, James. Hold on; I need to talk to you." "Yes, sir."

Kisen slides out from under Hope, trying not to wake her.

"Yes, sir. What can I do for you?"

"James, you've been with us since I was a kid, starting as Dad's butler, now with me. You've seen a couple of my girlfriends come and go. But James, I've never felt like this before. I really, really like her."

James smiles. "What are you asking me, sir?"

"I don't know, James. I guess I just need to vent. You're the one I've always come to when I need to talk."

James laughs. "I know. You always have since you were a kid."

"But I've never let you respond."

"Do you really want me to respond, sir?"

"Yes, I do."

"Then what are you asking me?"

"Can I have a relationship with the woman I own?"

"It's been done before, sir."

"I know, James, but I don't want her to be with me because she has to, because I own her. That's not what I want. I want her to be with me because she wants to be."

"Sir, you'll be able to tell, I assure you. All you have to do is ask. You'll know if she's telling the truth. But give her time to get to know you first, and you need time to get to know her."

"Good advice, James."

"Sir, may I speak honestly and openly?"

"Yes, that's what I'm asking you to do."

"Sir, you have a good soul. You've always been special; nothing like your father, nothing like your siblings. You've always treated us with respect and care, never looked at us differently or treated us badly. I'm so happy to be with you instead of your father or your siblings."

"That's because I picked you, James. I considered you my friend. Dad didn't want to let you go."

"Thank you, sir. But what I was going to say is I'm not surprised. You're a good man, but be careful; some white people may not understand."

"I know. Thank you, James."

"Would you like me to have the cooks fix you and your guest breakfast?"

"Yes, that would be good. Have them serve it in the dining room in about an hour."

Kisen wakes Hope with a kiss and shows her to the guest room so she can get dressed and ready for breakfast.

"Oh my, this room is beautiful."

"There's the shower, and here are some sweats you can put on. They're mine, so I know they'll be a little big. When you're finished, come down; someone will show you to the dining room."

Hope showers and gets dressed. She quietly leaves the guest room and makes her way downstairs, admiring the house. She reaches the kitchen and finds the cooks. They look up and smile at her. She smiles back. One of them takes her by the arm and leads her to the dining room where Master Kisen awaits. He gets up and pulls out her chair.

Kisen sits and tells the cooks it's okay to serve breakfast. Hope feels too nervous to eat, having never experienced this type of treatment before.

"Hope, I'm sorry."

"Why are you sorry, sir?"

"You're uncomfortable."

"It's not your fault. We're just from two different worlds, and I'm in yours right now. I don't know how to act."

"I invited you because I enjoy you. You don't have to act, just be yourself. Come on, let's eat so I can get you back to school."

The drive back to school is quiet, both thinking about the night before and how much they enjoyed being with each other. Kisen wonders again if she truly enjoys being with him or if it's only because he's her Master. That's why he's held back from making a move past a kiss.

Hope wonders where their relationship is going. She knows it's not up to her; it's whatever her Master decides. She's just a pawn at his mercy. If he doesn't want to see her anymore, it's up to him; after all, he owns her. They both want each other but hold back because they don't know how the other feels. Their feelings are growing. Neither one of them has thought about Akim; he's still in the picture.

Master Kisen suddenly stops in front of Hope's dorm. She opens the door.

"Kisen, thank you for last night. I had a wonderful time. You showed me a life I only imagined, never thought I would experience. You gave me a glimpse of your world, and I enjoyed it."

"Hope, shut the door. I'm going to tell you something, and you listen. I know I'm your Master, but I can't stop these feelings I'm developing for you. I think about you all the time. I want to be with you all the time. I don't know where I'm going with this, but I wanted you to know. I need to know if you spend time with me because you feel you have to, out of duty because I'm your Master, or because you want to. I need to know the truth."

Hope lays her hand on his. "Yes, it's true I go with you because you're my Master and I have to. But you have no control over my feelings, and my feelings say I'm enjoying our time together. Kisen, how could I not love it? So to answer your question, I love being with you. And that's the truth."

"Hope, will you do me one favor? Tell me if you ever feel uncomfortable with anything I ask of you."

"I'll try, but it's going to be hard. This life is the only life I've ever known. You are my Master, and I'm your slave. Kisen, have you forgotten that I have a boyfriend?"

"I haven't forgotten."

She sees in his eyes that he really cares about her. He is real, and she cares for him too. She asks him what he wants from her.

"I want you," he replies.

"You already have me." "I want your heart."

Kisen leans over and kisses her goodbye. "When's your last class?"

"Thursday."

"Can I come get you to spend the weekend with me? See, I asked."

Hope laughs. "Yes, I would love to spend the weekend with you." Kisen smiles and kisses her again. "Till this weekend."

Chapter 22
The New Addition

—◊◊◊—

Gabriel is at home catching up on information about the Underground, the upcoming presidential election, and plans to locate the facility that controls the chips. He knows he can't afford to buy his family's freedom and that Master Kisen won't allow it, they're too valuable, so their only chance is through the election. His thoughts are suddenly interrupted.

Gabriel hears the front door open, must be the kids coming home from school. He goes to see how their day went, especially Samuel; he's still grieving.

Destinee asks her father if they can talk, so he takes her to his office. She tells him she's ready to ask Master Kisen if he would buy Mercy.

"The family all agreed to help Mercy; now it's up to Master Kisen."

"Dad, I know you don't want me to ask him, but it's all I've been thinking about. I want to help her, please."

He replies that he doesn't think Master Kisen will do it. "You're asking for a lot."

"I know, Daddy, but he's kind."

"Go."

"Really?"

"I said go."

Destinee hugs him and runs to her room. She lies on her bed and reaches under her pillow for her phone.

"Hello, Master Kisen."

"Hello, Destinee. What can I do for you?"

"I know I'm not supposed to ask, but I'm just a kid; I don't know better. I want to ask a big favor."

"How big is it?"

"It's really big, sir."

"Go ahead. It won't hurt to ask."

"Do you remember Mercy, my roommate at reform school? The girl who took care of me, the one who talked sense to me."

"Yes, I remember."

"Can we have her?"

"What do you mean, 'have her'?"

"Sir, she doesn't have anyone. She's all alone. I promise I'll make sure she behaves. She'll be a good investment. We'll both be class 5 one day."

Master Kisen laughs. "How do you know you can achieve class 5, and how do you know she can?"

"We'll work hard, I promise."

"How does the rest of the family feel?"

"I checked with them. We discussed it. They all agreed if you said yes."

"You're asking a lot, Destinee. She's in reform school."

"So was I. But I was there because I deserved it; she didn't. She's there through no fault of her own."

"Master Kisen, she was good to me. She's my friend. I just want her to have a chance at a better life. Besides, you're rich, really rich."

"You're very thoughtful. It appears you have changed."

"I have, thanks to you and Mercy."

"Tell you what: I'll think about it, but I'm not making any promises."

"Thank you, sir."

"I said I'd think about it, so don't get your hopes up."

"I know, sir. At least you didn't say no."

"Her master may not want to sell her."

"I thought about that. I'll pray on it. Thank you, sir."

Destinee runs downstairs. "Daddy, Master Kisen said he'd think about it."

"I told you we were friends."

At that moment Jessie walks in and hears the conversation. "Stop saying he's your friend. He's not; he's your master. If he were your friend, he'd set you free. Why don't you ask him that? Ask him to free your whole family. Then you can call him your friend."

"Yes, Mama." Destinee goes back to her room.

Jessie asks Gabriel if he really thinks Master Kisen will buy Mercy just because Destinee asked. He tells her that if he does, they'll have to prepare. Gabriel asks if she's sure she's ready for an addition to the family so soon after losing Seth.

"Yes. I'm ready. This little girl needs a family; she's had a rough life. Let's give her a chance."

Meanwhile, Master Kisen calls his personal assistant and asks her to contact the reform school for Mercy's master's name and number. Once he has the information, he calls Gabriel to make sure they're all right with this before he contacts Mercy's master. After speaking with Gabriel, he makes the call.

He first introduces himself to Mercy's master, who already knows of him and his family, owners of one of the richest families in the country. He explains what happened between Destinee and Mercy at reform school, expresses gratitude, and makes his offer to purchase Mercy.

"Do you always buy slaves for your slaves?" the man asks Kisen.

"No. I'm not purchasing a slave for a slave. What are your plans for Mercy, may I ask?"

"Mr. Brown, Mercy means a lot to me. I have plans for her."

"I see. She means a lot to you, that's why she's been in reform school all these years instead of getting a good education?"

"I put her there till she's ripe," he says with a chuckle.

"I plan to put her in the bordello with her momma. She's cute; she'll bring in a lot of money."

"Why didn't you consider sending her to university? You may have a class 4 or 5 on your hands."

"I don't have time for that. I want my money now. I know who you are; I've heard of your family, owners of big corporations and thousands of slaves. Normal people don't have the ability, time, or money to waste on long-term investments."

"Then sell her to me and don't worry why I want to buy her."

"OK, OK. I'll have to think about how much I'd lose by selling her. I'll get back to you later today."

"No. We're doing this now. I don't have the time."

Kisen is a businessman; he knows if he gives the man time to think, he'll come back with a ridiculous demand. So the negotiation begins. It goes on for 30 minutes before they reach an agreement on Mercy's worth. Kisen ends up paying more than the going rate for a 15-year-old slave girl with low-class parents.

The purchase is made for $50,000. Her master tried for $100,000 but settled, arguing he would earn much more from the bordello while she was in her prime. Kisen's counter was how long that would take versus money in hand now. The man couldn't pass on that.

Kisen immediately calls Gabriel with the good news: they have a new addition to the household, he'll bring Mercy over tonight, and he'll add money to Gabriel's account to cover expenses.

Gabriel and Jesse decide not to tell Destinee. They want it to be a surprise when Master Kisen brings Mercy. They find themselves a little excited. Jesse decides to cook a special dinner and bake a cake.

Gabriel takes charge of cleaning. He has Destinee tidy her room and change her sheets, and he straightens up Hope's room for Mercy until he can order another bed for Destinee's.

Gabriel knocks on Samuel's door before entering. He finds him at his computer playing games. Samuel is starting to adjust to life without his brother. Gabriel tells him about Mercy moving in and asks how he feels about it. Samuel says he's fine, that he'll have to adjust but can do it, and that he's proud of Destinee for caring about someone other than herself. He's noticed a positive change in her.

Master Kisen arrives at the reform school to pick up Mercy. She's never been outside the facility since she arrived at 8 years old; now she's 15. The headmaster hands Kisen her file, containing everything about her, grades, family, and ancestry.

Gabriel asks, "Does she know what's going on or where she's going?"

"No, sir. All she knows is that you purchased her from her master. Nothing else. It's up to you what you want her to know."

Mercy is brought into the office.

"Mercy, this is your new master. Remember everything you've learned here, and be a good girl."

"Yes, sir."

"Hello, Mercy."

"Hello, sir."

Mercy keeps her head down, as she's been taught, only speak when spoken to and never make eye contact. She climbs into the back seat, not knowing where she's going. She expects the worst, wondering what horrors await when the car stops. She's heard terrible stories from others about their masters and white people in general. She thinks, Oh my, I'm going to be a whore. She starts to cry.

Kisen hears her sniffles. "Are you crying?"

"Yes, sir."

"Why?"

"I don't want to be a whore."

"A what?"

"A whore."

Kisen bursts out laughing. "You think that's where I'm taking you?"

"Yes, sir."

"Mercy, I assure you, you're not going to a whorehouse." He laughs again.

"Stop crying and enjoy the scenery. I hear this is your first time out of the reform school."

"Yes, sir, it is."

Mercy wipes her eyes and looks out the window. The city lights are beautiful. She studies the people in passing cars, mostly Black, some white, and notices many police cars. She feels a little better knowing she's not going to a bordello, but she's still nervous.

Kisen pulls up to a two-story brick house with a flower garden. Mercy thinks it's beautiful. She's only seen houses like this in books. She remembers living in a crowded low-income apartment building as a little girl.

"Come on, grab your things. This is your new home."

Gabriel is waiting at the door. He opens it and invites them in.

"Hello, Gabriel."

"Hello, Master Kisen. Hello, Mercy."

Gabriel introduces her to Jesse.

"Hello, Mercy. Welcome to the family."

Jesse hugs her. Mercy hugs her back nervously. She's never felt a hug before, except when she and Destinee hugged goodbye. She wonders if she'll ever see her friend again.

"Well, Mercy, time to meet the rest of the family," Jesse says.

"Kids, come on down, dinner's almost ready."

Destinee runs downstairs. First she sees Master Kisen, then Mercy. They stare at each other in disbelief before running into each other's arms, hugging and crying.

"I knew it! I knew he would buy you."

"He's your master?"

"Yes, now he's yours too."

"You really asked him to buy me, and he did?"

"Yes, he did."

She looks at her father. "I told you he would." Then at her mother.

"I told you he's my friend."

Destinee walks up to Master Kisen. "Thank you, sir. I'll make you proud." She glances at Mercy.

"We both will."

Master Kisen calls them over. "Girls, sit down. Mercy, Destinee asked me to buy you, and she made promises I expect you both to keep. Keep your grades up, stay out of trouble. Mercy, you were very expensive, more than I'd normally pay. Don't make me regret it."

"I won't, sir," Mercy says.

Master Kisen turns to leave. Destinee runs after him and touches his hand. He turns, and she hugs him. Everyone gasps, including Mercy. He freezes, then hugs her back.

"Thank you, sir. You've made us both happy."

Mercy walks up too. "Sir, thank you for giving me a chance. I promise you won't regret it."

Kisen turns and walks out, while Gabriel and Jesse stand there in shock at the hug Destinee gave him.

Chapter 23
Mercy Adjusting

———ᴧᴧᴧ———

The whole family takes part in helping Mercy adjust to her new life. Her first night is spent with Destinee showing her around the house and the room they'll share. While fixing Mercy's hair, Destinee tells her about their school and friends. She finds an outfit for Mercy to wear tomorrow, and they plan to go shopping for clothes and necessities.

"I've never had new clothes. I've never had anything of my own before."

"Well, that's going to change. You're going to love it here."

"I already do."

Destinee shows Mercy Hope's room. "You can sleep here till we get you a bed. Then you'll be my roommate again." Mercy looks worried, and Destinee notices.

"What's wrong? You don't like it?"

"No, that's not it."

"Then what is it?"

"I'm afraid to sleep alone."

"Come on, you can sleep with me."

They lie in bed, both too excited to sleep.

"Destinee, are you asleep?"

"No, I can't sleep."

"I can't either. Thank you for doing this for me."

"I did it for me too. I needed you. You're going to be a wonderful sister."

Morning comes quickly, since the girls barely slept. They get dressed and run downstairs for breakfast.

"Mercy, Destinee's clothes fit you perfectly, and your hair is so cute."

"Thank you, Mrs. Brown. Destinee did it."

"Destinee, you did a beautiful job."

"I know I did," she says with a smile.

"Hurry up and eat, girls, so we can go shopping."

"Shopping? We're not going to school?"

"Not today. Master Kisen gave us the day off and a debit card to buy what Mercy needs."

Mercy is excited. She's never had new clothes before, only that drab gray uniform.

Samuel sits down to breakfast without speaking or acknowledging anyone. Jesse looks at him. "Well, good morning, Samuel."

"Good morning."

"Samuel, this is Mercy. Mercy, this is Samuel," Jesse says.

"Hello," says Mercy.

Samuel glances at her, nods, and leaves to catch the bus.

"He's been like that since we lost our brother," Destinee says.

Gabriel walks into the kitchen, grabs a slice of toast, kisses his wife, then kisses Destinee on the forehead before heading to the door. He stops, turns back, walks over to Mercy, and kisses her forehead too, then leaves for work.

Mercy and Destinee smile at each other. Mercy has never been kissed on the forehead before; in fact, never kissed at all. She feels it's an acknowledgment that she's welcome in the family, and she likes it.

Chapter 24
Surprise for Hope

———

Hope had been calling Akim for days, but he hadn't answered or returned her calls. She'd left messages, but nothing. He usually met her in the library, but he hadn't shown up, so she decided to go to his dorm room and knocked on his door. His roommate answered and said Akim wasn't there and didn't know where he was.

Akim suddenly appeared around the corner. Not expecting to see her, he tried to back up, but it was too late; she saw him.

"Akim, why haven't you returned my calls? I was worried."

"You didn't look worried when you took off with that white man the other night."

"Akim, that was my Master. I accidentally left my phone, so I couldn't call you."

"Why was he picking you up so late? You didn't come back until the next day."

"Akim, I called you when I got back."

"You stayed out with him all night. Why? What did you do?"

"Nothing. He just wanted to talk, and we didn't pay attention to the time. So, I stayed on the plantation, but nothing happened. Kisen's not like that."

"Kisen? You call your Master by his name?"

"I mean Master Kisen."

"What's going on, Hope?"

"Nothing's going on. He's a different kind of Master, nothing like his father. He's kind, he treats his slaves well, and he enjoys my company. He wants to be friends."

"Friends? He owns you. How can you be friends? Tell you what, if you're such good friends, tell him to set you free. You ask him that, then give me a call. I need time to think. My girl stayed out all night with her Master and 'accidentally' left her phone behind."

Akim turned and walked away as Hope watched him go.

"I love you, Akim," she called.

He turned back. "Hope, do you realize you've never said those three words to me? Never. So why now?"

"Do you love me, or do you love this plan we devised together?"

"Never mind, Hope. Don't answer that, I already know."

Akim turned and walked down the hall to his room, slamming the door in anger.

Hope walked back to her room, thinking about what Akim had just said. Was it true? She wondered if she really loved him or just the idea of buying their freedom together and moving to Paris. Her mind drifted to her night with Kisen, the way he made her feel, feelings Akim had never given her. She couldn't wait for the weekend to see Kisen again.

She reached her room and lay on her bed. Finals were done, she had nothing to do, Akim was mad at her, and her roommate had left. She wanted to call Kisen but knew she was getting too comfortable. She kept telling herself he was her Master, even though it didn't feel like a Master–Slave relationship. It was so exciting.

Finally, she got the nerve to call Kisen. After all, what did she have to lose? She dialed all but the last number and hung up, again and again, until finally she let it ring.

Kisen answered on the first ring. "Hello, Hope. Wow, you've been thinking about me," he laughed.

"To what do I owe the pleasure of this call?"

"I don't know. I know I shouldn't be doing this…"

"You don't know, and you shouldn't be doing what?" he laughed.

"Didn't I give you a pass, Sweetie?"

"Yes," she said timidly.

"I didn't have anything to do. My finals are done, so I thought I'd call just to say hello."

"I'm glad you did. That means you like me after all. My day's free too, want to start our weekend early?"

"I'd love to," she said with a smile.

"If you want to."

"Good. I want to. I'm ready to see you. I'll move the arrangements up and be there in three hours."

"I'll start packing."

"You don't have to pack anything. Whatever you need, I got you, babe."

"Nothing?"

"Nothing but your ID."

"I'll call you when I'm out front."

"OK," she said excitedly.

Hope hung up, wondering what he had planned. She was so excited and happy she wanted to tell someone, but who? Her best friend was Akim, and she couldn't tell him. She realized she didn't feel guilty about Akim at all. Maybe he was right about her not loving him.

Her thoughts were interrupted by the phone ringing. It was Akim.

She didn't want to answer, afraid it would kill her mood, but she did.

"Hello?"

"Hey Hope, we need to talk. I'm on my way over."

"Not now, Akim. It's not a good time. I'm going home; I have some thinking to do."

"OK. I'll give you time to think. We'll talk when you get back. Goodbye, Hope."

The call did kill her mood. She started to feel guilty about Akim but was still so excited about seeing Kisen. She realized she'd never felt this way before; these were new feelings, and she liked them.

Three hours flew by. Hope, excited, went downstairs. She opened the door, and there he was already, sitting with a big smile. He'd driven the truck with tinted windows again, so she had no choice but to sit next to him. She climbed in with the biggest smile on her face.

"What are you smiling about?" he asked.

"I don't know… I guess I'm happy."

"Where are we going, may I ask?"

"It's a surprise. Don't you graduate next weekend?"

"Yes."

"Consider it an early graduation present."

"A present?"

"Yes. Hope you like it."

She realized no one had ever given her a present before except her parents. Not even Akim, aside from his paintings, and those were never surprises; she always knew what she was getting.

They drove almost three hours, and Hope realized they were close to the plantation. Kisen pulled off to the side of the road. He told her to turn around so he could put a blindfold on her, then continued driving.

"We're almost there."

They came to a stop, and she heard the door open. "Is she ready?" she heard Kisen ask someone.

"Hello Master Kisen, yes, she's ready, sir."

Kisen took Hope by the hand and led her up some stairs. She could tell they were outside, the air brushed through her hair.

"Be careful, this is your last step."

He led her inside and sat her down. "Leave the blindfold on. I'll be right back."

She heard movement and whispers, but had no idea where she was. Still, she trusted him and knew she was safe. Soon he returned and sat beside her.

"Are you ready to take the blindfold off?"

"Yes, I'm ready."

"Wait a minute." He leaned over, kissed her softly on the lips, then removed the blindfold.

She looked around and gasped. "Oh my God… I'm on a plane! I've never been on a plane before. But you know that," she added with a smile. Suddenly nerves hit her; she was scared.

Kisen saw it. "Calm down, there's nothing to be afraid of. I've flown hundreds of times. You're safe."

"Where are we going?"

"Can't tell you; it'll spoil the surprise. Put your seat belt on, we're about to take off."

Kisen told the pilots he was ready. As the engines roared, he grabbed her hand. "It's alright, I got you."

Fear washed over her, yet she felt safe with Kisen. The plane began rolling. She squeezed his hand and closed her eyes as they lifted off.

"Come on, open your eyes. Look out the window, you don't want to miss this."

She peeked out, watching as the ground shrank below. "Oh my God… oh my God. The lights are beautiful down there."

"Yes, they are. Feeling better?"

"Yes."

"Good. Just enjoy. Want a drink to calm your nerves?"

"Yes, that would be nice."

"A glass of wine?"

"Yes."

"Red, white, or rosé?"

"I don't know, I've never had wine."

"Then why'd you say yes?"

"Because you said it would calm my nerves. I need my nerves calmed."

Kisen called for wine. "Bring me red, white, and rosé."

The stewardess brought three bottles and glasses, setting them down.

"Thank you."

"You say thank you to your slaves?" Hope asked.

"Yes, I do."

"Are you sure your father raised you?"

"Yes, but I have my own way of thinking, not his."

He told her to try each. She tasted the white, then the red, then the rosé.

"I like the rosé."

Kisen poured her a glass. Two glasses later, Hope was lightheaded, starting to doze. Kisen noticed.

"Come on, let's get some sleep. We'll be there in a few hours, and I want you ready for your surprise."

"You mean this isn't it? My first airplane ride?"

Kisen laughed. "No, sweetie. There's more to come. This is only the beginning."

"I'm so excited, I don't know if I can sleep."

"Come on, you can lay in my arms."

Hope curled into him, comfortable, like she belonged there. Within minutes, she was fast asleep. He kissed her forehead and drifted off with her.

Morning came quickly. The stewardess gently woke Kisen. "Sir, we're about to land. You need to return to your seats and fasten your belts."

"OK, thank you."

She smiled, secretly thinking how lucky Hope was. She had never seen Master Kisen with a Black woman before, and this one was so beautiful.

Kisen leaned over and kissed Hope on the cheek. "Come on, we need to sit for landing."

Hope sat, and Kisen fastened her belt. Looking out the window, she whispered, "Look at the clouds, they're beautiful."

"Keep looking."

He had arranged the landing so she'd see the Eiffel Tower. As the plane descended, the landmark appeared.

"Oh my God, it's the Eiffel Tower!" she screamed, then blushed.

"Oh, I'm sorry."

Kisen laughed. "That's alright, you can scream."

"You brought me to Paris."

"SURPRISE!" he grinned.

"This is your graduation present."

"Are you serious?"

"Yes. Just look out the window."

Hope burst into tears.

"Why are you crying, babe?"

"I'm so happy. This was a dream I never thought would come true, and you made it real. Thank you so much." Kisen smiled.

"I'm not done yet."

The plane landed. Hope hastily unbuckled and hugged him. "Thank you, this is the best gift anyone's ever given me. I still can't believe you did this."

"Hope, you deserve it."

They exited the plane hand in hand. She tried to pull away, but he held tighter.

"You don't have to. We're in Paris, remember? No slaves here."

"Oh my, I forgot."

They climbed into a limo. Hope took his hand. "This feels like a dream."

"The dream is just starting," Kisen said, kissing her hand.

The limo stopped in the most affluent part of Paris. Hope was stunned, taking in the scenery. The car pulled up to the most beautiful hotel she had ever seen; something out of a magazine.

The driver opened the door. To her surprise, he was white. Hope had never seen a white man working. He reached for her hand and helped her out, smiling warmly. She couldn't believe it, a white man helped her.

They walk into the lobby and Hope freezes in amazement. The walls are white trimmed with gold, the floors white marble, and beautiful chandeliers hang everywhere. She thinks to herself, Is this what heaven looks like?

They enter the elevator, mirrored walls, a glass door, and gold buttons. Kisen reserved the Penthouse Suite, so the elevator stops on the top floor. The bellboy opens the door for Hope and Kisen. She starts to walk behind them, as she's been trained to do, but Kisen grabs her hand and pulls her up to walk beside him.

"You have to get used to being in Paris, young lady." She smiles.

"I know. I'm trying."

The bellboy opens the suite door. Hope walks in, amazed by what she sees, then steps onto the balcony. To her astonishment, she's facing the Eiffel Tower. She begins to cry.

Kisen joins her. "Why are you crying now?"

"What can I say, overjoyed, happy, amazed, bliss. I don't know. I can't put into words what I'm feeling. I've never experienced joy like this before."

"Baby, you're going to experience much, much more this weekend."

"Why are you doing this for me?"

"You told me your dream was to go to Paris but thought it would never happen. I wanted to prove you wrong, be the one to make your dream come true."

"I really like you, Kisen."

"And I really like you too, Hope."

"You know this is a free country. Are you going to run?" he asks with a smile.

"If you'd asked me that two weeks ago, I might have tried. But the time I've spent with you has been the best of my life, more than I could have dreamed. How could I run from you?"

"That's what I wanted to hear."

Kisen takes her by the hand and leads her to the dressing room. He opens the door to reveal clothes, shoes, lingerie, jewelry, perfume, everything she could possibly need.

Hope whispers in his ear, "Pinch me."

"Why would I do that?"

"I just want to make sure I'm not dreaming." She pauses.

"Never mind. Don't pinch me, if I am dreaming, I don't want to wake up."

He lifts her chin so their lips meet, kissing her passionately.

"Come on, sweetie. We have a city to explore."

"What should I wear?"

"Something comfortable. We're going to do a lot of walking."

They disappear into their separate dressing rooms. Hope walks around, admiring the clothes and jewelry, smelling the colognes. She steps into the shower, sampling the body washes until she picks one. The warm water feels amazing, and the scent fills the room.

Suddenly, a knock at the door.

"Can I join you?"

She's nervous but says yes. He's her master, and look what he's done for her.

Kisen opens the door and climbs into the shower. Hope stands with her back to him, too nervous to turn around. He smiles; it's cute. He takes the rag from her hand and washes her back, then gently turns her around and washes her all over, admiring her perfect body. He washes her hair.

"Keep your eyes closed while I rinse you."

He grabs a towel, dries her off, wraps it around her, and carries her to the bed. "Babe, you can open your eyes." He removes the towel and rubs lotion over her body. They're both excited, wanting each other, but Kisen wants to be sure she wants him too. He won't take her because he owns her; he wants her to choose him.

He lays her on the bed, then turns to leave. She's puzzled. "You don't want to?" she asks.

"Yes, I want you bad; can't you tell? But not like that. You let me know when you want me."

"Get dressed." He leaves her room and shuts the door.

She lays there thinking about what he said: Let him know when I want him.

Hope gets dressed, short khaki skirt, white halter top, white tennis shoes. She decides to wear her hair down. Usually, she wears it in a bun, but she tries something new. Her long black wavy hair touches her waist. She applies a little makeup and sprays on some cologne. She takes one final look in the floor-length mirror, barely recognizing herself after wearing drab gray all her life.

She slowly opens the door. Kisen, sitting on the couch, sees her peeking out and laughs. "Come on out, let me see you."

Hope steps out slowly, blushing.

He stands, gazing at her beauty, speechless.

"Am I alright?" she asks.

"No. You're not alright; you're the most beautiful woman I've ever seen."

"The most beautiful black woman?"

"No. Like I said, you're the most beautiful woman I've ever seen. Why do you try to hide it?"

"I didn't know. I never thought I was beautiful, especially wearing that gray."

"Babe, you made that gray look good."

"I can't believe you don't realize how beautiful you are."

Kisen goes into her dressing room and comes out with jewelry, a diamond pendant he places around her neck, bracelets for her wrists, and rings for her fingers.

"Why didn't you put any jewelry on?"

"I've never worn jewelry before. Have you forgotten what I am? We don't have such luxuries."

"You do now." This shakes Kisen and brings him back to reality.

"I'm sorry, babe. I almost forgot. This feels so normal to me." Kisen brings her over to the mirror.

"You look beautiful."

"Come on, let's start our day. We have so much to do and see."

Kisen proudly walks her through the lobby, knowingly holding the hand of the most beautiful woman in the hotel. Their first stop is a small corner restaurant for breakfast. They then stroll through the streets of Paris, making their way to the Eiffel Tower and taking a boat ride down the Seine for lunch.

It's mid-afternoon. Kisen takes her hand. "Would you like to explore more or get some rest before dinner?"

"Let's get some rest. We can do the Louvre and the Palace of Versailles tomorrow."

"Let's go. Do you want me to call the limo?"

"No, let's walk. It's not far."

Kisen takes her hand. She loves holding it; she feels safe with him, a warm feeling consuming her whole body. She's never felt like this before, and she doesn't want it to stop.

They reach the room. Hope goes out on the balcony and looks over the city she's always dreamed of visiting. Kisen joins her and takes her hand.

She squeezes it. "Did you notice? No one stared at us, no one paid attention. We blended right in; it felt so normal. Everyone here is so nice. It's not like this in America. Most white people there are so mean, except you, of course."

Kisen smiles. "This is a nice place."

94

"Why are you doing this for me?"

"I told you, it's your graduation gift."

"Kisen, masters don't do things like this for their slaves. Why are you so nice to me?"

"Because I like you, Hope. I like you a lot." Hope smiles.

"I like you a lot too."

"You get some rest. I'm going to step out for about an hour. I'll be back. If you need anything, just hit that buzzer."

"Okay."

He kisses her on the cheek.

Hope steps out on the balcony and lies on the couch, staring up at the clouds, thinking about how all the things she dreamed about are coming true, more than she expected, much more. The way she's treated here is nothing like America. People aren't looking down on her like she's property, a commodity. She wonders how she can go back to that life after experiencing this. She'd love to tell Akim about her experiences, but she knows she can't; he wouldn't understand. She wishes she could tell her parents, but she can't. How would they react? Hope falls asleep with the biggest smile on her face, feeling like a princess.

Kisen returns from running errands. He walks around the suite, looking for Hope. She's not in her dressing room, not in her bedroom, not in the bathroom. Did she run? he wonders. He walks out onto the balcony, not expecting to see her asleep on the couch. He laughs softly, relieved. He stands over her, thinking how beautiful she is, how much he loves her company, how he loves making her smile. But he wonders where this will end up. Right now, he doesn't care; he loves the moment he's in.

He caresses her face with the back of his hand. "Come on, sweetie, let's get dressed for dinner. Your dress is hanging on the back of your door, and your shoes are under it. I'll go to my dressing room and get dressed." He helps her up and walks her to her dressing room.

After she showers, she holds up the dress, stunned by its beauty. She's never seen anything like it, a red floor-length gown, low cut at the front, exposing the top of her breasts, with a low-cut back down to her waist and a long slit showing her right leg. The shoes are high-heeled gold sandals, matching the gold polish Kisen picked out at the nail salon earlier that day. That was also a first for Hope, having a white woman give her a manicure and pedicure.

Hope puts her hair up in a bun on top of her head with ringlets framing her face, a style she's practiced so many times only to take it down again, with nowhere to go. She puts on the jewelry he laid out for her, a diamond necklace, earrings, bracelet, and ring. She sprays cologne on her neck, chest, and wrists. She not only feels like a princess, she looks like one. She's never worn red before, never worn anything so beautiful.

She walks to the door and peeks out, seeing Kisen sitting on the couch. He hears the door open and looks up. "Come on out, don't be shy."

She steps out slowly.

"Oh my God, baby, you are beautiful."

"How did you know my size?"

"You're about the same size as my sister, a size six, and I looked at your shoe size."

"I need to get you one more thing."

Kisen walks into her dressing room and comes out with a tube of lipstick, applying it to her lips. "You've never worn lipstick, have you?"

"No."

"You have beautiful full lips. Let's show them off. You don't need anything else; you look absolutely stunning."

"And you are very handsome, sir."

Kisen is wearing a black custom-made suit with a red silk shirt, the top buttons open, showing his chest hair.

"Let's do this, sweetie."

Kisen takes her hand, kisses it, and leads her out the door.

As they exit the elevator, everyone in the lobby stops and stares at the beautiful couple.

Hope whispers to Kisen, "Why is everyone staring at us?"

"Because you're beautiful."

"Maybe it's because you're handsome."

"Maybe it's both," he says with a smile.

The limo ride is short. The driver opens the door, reaches out his hand, and helps Hope out. She steps out and looks up at the Eiffel Tower, amazed. It's lit with sparkling lights, breathtaking. Kisen takes her hand and leads her to the elevator.

When they reach the top, the door opens to reveal a candlelit dinner, musicians playing, waiters and waitresses standing by ready to serve. She has never seen white people serving, and smiling too. A waiter pulls out her chair. Tears roll down her face.

Kisen wipes her tears with a napkin. "Why the tears?"

"I'm so happy. Never in my wildest dreams would I expect something like this. This is why you left today, isn't it?"

"Yes. I had to make arrangements to rent this."

"You rented the Eiffel Tower for me?"

"Yes. Told you I had a lot more surprises."

They enjoy their dinner, listening to music and taking in the cityscape of lights all around them. Hope wonders how things can go back to the way they were after experiencing this together. She wonders if he treats all his women this way.

Kisen notices her expression. "What's wrong, Hope? I see you."

"Are you wondering how things will go back to the way they were when we return to America?"

"Yes. How did you know?"

"Because I've been thinking the same thing. I want you to know it doesn't have to go back, unless you want it to."

"Hope, I won't let it go back."

"Kisen, you can't stop it."

"Watch me. I want you. I've been falling for you since the day I brought Destinee home. You were walking down the stairs; I couldn't take my eyes off you. I know we're from two different worlds, but I can't help how I feel about you. I know your body belongs to me, but I want your heart, and I want you to give it to me freely."

Tears swell in Hope's eyes. She doesn't know what to say. She realizes she hasn't thought about Akim, and he's never made her feel like this.

"Do you think you could care for me, Hope? Or is it too soon?"

"I already do. But I'm afraid. How will we carry this on when we go back home?"

"Let's not think about that now. Let's just enjoy our time here, enjoy each other."

They finish the night driving around the city, enjoying the sights and each other while sipping champagne.

When they return to the room, Kisen puts on soft music while Hope sits on the balcony admiring the city. She can't get enough of its beauty. Kisen steps out and begins taking her picture.

"I have to capture this moment."

"You had pictures taken while we were having dinner."

"I know, but I didn't take them."

Kisen hands Hope a glass of wine. "Let's make a toast, to us and our future together."

They toast and kiss.

"Come on, babe, let's dance."

"I don't know how to dance," she whispers in his ear.

"Well, I guess I'll have to teach you."

They spend the night drinking, laughing, and dancing. Kisen slowly unzips her dress; it falls to the floor. She steps out of it, revealing a red lace bustier. He runs his hands through her hair, letting it fall.

He whispers in her ear, "You are a vision of beauty. I love you. Give me your heart, Hope."

Hope whispers back, "I think I'm falling in love with you, and you already have it. Kisen, I'm ready to give myself to you. I want you."

They share a passionate kiss. Kisen picks her up and carries her to his bed. They lie there holding each other, kissing deeply. He begins to undress her, then himself. He explores her body with his hands, then his mouth, kissing her everywhere. She lies back, enjoying his touch.

He looks up at her. "Do I have your permission to make love to you, Hope?"

"Yes, Kisen. You have my permission. I want you as much as you want me."

As he begins to make love to her, he realizes she's a virgin and stops.

"Why did you stop?"

"You're a virgin."

"I know."

"This is your first time?"

"I know that too." She laughs softly.

"But you have a boyfriend."

"We never made love. He never attempted."

"Why not? You're beautiful; how could he resist? I had a hard time resisting."

"Kisen, are we going to talk all night, or are we going to do this? I want you to be my first, and my last."

She reaches up, grabs him, and pulls him into her. They make love, while falling in love.

"Hope, things are not going back to the way they were. You know that, don't you?"

"That's up to you. You know I have no control."

"Come on, baby. We need to get some sleep. We have more adventures tomorrow."

They spend the night in each other's arms, trying to sleep but finding it hard to do.

Morning comes fast. Kisen wrapped up their trip by visiting the Louvre Museum, having lunch while sailing down the Seine River again, and attending a show at the Moulin Rouge. They ended their night making love.

Sunday morning arrives, and Kisen has one last adventure planned before catching their plane. Hope wakes up happy and in love.

"Good morning, sweetie. I have one last surprise for you."

"Another?"

"Yes, one more. Now let's get dressed; we have to hurry and catch a train."

They both dress quickly and head to the train station. The trip is short, about 45 minutes. They arrive in the town of Versailles. After walking about a block, they're standing in front of the Palace of Versailles.

"Oh my, it's beautiful. I know the history of this palace; I learned about it in school."

"Would you like a tour?"

"Yes, please."

After touring the palace, the gardens, and the fountains, they catch the train back to Paris and then head to the airport.

"What about packing?"

"Everything you need is packed. Your gifts will be at the plantation waiting for you. I couldn't have them delivered to your house; how could you explain them to your parents?"

"You're so right."

"Everything is yours."

"But you know I can't wear them in America. I have to go back to that hideous grey."

They arrive at the plane. The white chauffeur opens the door and takes Hope by the hand.

"Come on, young lady."

She thinks, This is never going to happen again, especially in America.

Hope watches out the window as the beautiful city disappears below the clouds. Last, she sees the Eiffel Tower vanish into the mist. Her eyes fill with tears. Kisen notices, takes her hand, and she lays her head on his shoulder.

"I don't want to leave; I love it here."

"We'll be back, I promise. I have so much more to show you, Rome, Egypt, Greece, much, much more."

"How can you promise such a thing?"

"I made this happen, didn't I? You are mine, and I can take you anywhere I want to. But I don't want to take you as my slave; I want to take you as my woman, the woman I love. So stop worrying. Your life is about to change, if you want it… if you want me."

Chapter 25
Back to America

Kisen and Hope slept all the way home, exhausted from their trip. Hope is awakened by a kiss on the cheek.

"Wake up, babe, we're home."

Hope is visibly upset, overcome with anxiety and dread. Kisen holds her.

"Come on, babe, I got you. Everything is going to be alright, I promise."

As they exit the plane, tears fill her eyes. After experiencing freedom in Paris, breathing the air in America feels like it's choking her. Kisen takes her hands, she pulls away. He takes it again, and they walk to his truck. He goes around and opens the door for her. She begins to cry again.

"Hope, why are you crying?"

"How are we going to do this? I know it's easy for you, this is the world you live in, but it's going to be hard for me."

"I told you, we're not going back to the way it was before. I love you, and we're going to make this work. Trust me."

The drive to school is quiet, filled with memories of Paris. Both are lost in thought.

They arrive at Hope's dorm and just sit there, looking at each other. Kisen takes her hand.

"Hope, nothing has changed between us. Only our location has changed. I loved you in Paris, and I still love you."

Kisen leans over to kiss her goodbye, but she stops him.

"We can't."

"Why can't we? Don't you belong to me?"

"Yes, I do, but you told me not to do anything that made me uncomfortable. I'd be uncomfortable kissing you in front of my dorm."

"You're right. I did say that."

"Goodbye, babe. All the things in Paris are yours, but I'll hold on to them since you're moving out of the dorm this week."

"OK. And thank you for the best time of my life. I'll hold on to these memories forever."

Kisen hands Hope a picture of them at the Eiffel Tower. She looks at it and tears roll again.

"I see it, but it still feels like a dream. Did this really happen?"

"Yes it did, babe. And there will be more."

"Okay, if you say so."

"I'll see you next weekend."

"Next weekend?"

"Your graduation."

"Oh, that's right," Hope says with a smile.

"My memories of Paris have pushed all my other memories to the back of my mind."

She leans over, kisses him anyway, and smiles.

"Thank you. Right now I'm the happiest person in the world."

"Babe, I'm not done making you happy. There are more happy memories coming your way."

"Good night, Kisen."

Hope gets out and walks up the steps to her dorm. Kisen sits there and watches her go inside, along with someone else, Akim.

Chapter 26
Claudette

It's Monday morning, and this is Mercy's first day of school. She stands in front of the mirror, amazed at how cute she looks. She never imagined this pretty girl was hidden behind that drab grey uniform and nappy hair. She likes what she sees: a new outfit, braids going back into a long ponytail down her back. Her hair has never been flat ironed before.

"Come on, girl, get out of the mirror. You know you cute," laughs Destinee.

They walk to the bus stop. Mercy feels nervous, Destinee sees it on her face and pats her on the back.

"You'll be fine. I'm here for you, girl."

"This is funny," says Destinee.

"What's funny?" asks Mercy.

"You're feeling like I did on my first day at the reform school."

"Hey, Destinee, who's this?" asks one of Destinee's friends.

Destinee looks at Mercy and smiles.

"She's my sister."

"I didn't know you had another sister."

"I didn't, but I do now. She lives with us."

Mercy feels proud hearing Destinee refer to her as her sister. She still can't believe how her life has turned out, and she owes it to Destinee.

"Destinee, I'm going to make you proud."

Mercy's first day is filled with testing to determine her learning level. Surprisingly, she turns out to be very intelligent, which means she'll attend classes with Destinee. They're both overjoyed at the news.

On the bus ride home, Mercy tells Destinee how much she enjoyed attending a real school and meeting her friends.

"Thank you for bringing me into your family and giving me a chance for a real life."

"Thank you for opening my eyes and saving me."

"I guess we saved each other," Mercy whispers in her ear.

When they arrive home, Mercy asks to use Destinee's computer to look up her mother. Destinee offers to help.

"What's her name?" Destinee asks. "Her name is Claudette Campbell."

Destinee enters the name into the slave database and locates Claudette Campbell. She is still alive and resides in a bordello owned by her Master. It's been eight years since Mercy last saw her mother.

"It's not right that she's there. It wasn't her fault."

"I know. She had a bad Master, not like Master Kisen."

"I know. He's cute too," says Mercy, and they start to giggle.

"Do you think he would buy her?"

"I don't know. Let's not push it, he just bought you."

"Do you think I could visit her?"

"I don't think that would be a good idea. Remember what he said, we need to be good and not get into any trouble."

"I know."

"I heard the boys at school talking about those places. They said the women there are beautiful, so your mother must be beautiful."

"I don't remember."

"You really want to see her, don't you?"

"Yes, but I don't want to get in trouble."

"Maybe we can sneak and go one day after school, as long as we're back before Mom and Dad get home. It's not very far."

"Can we go tomorrow?"

"We'll see."

The evening goes by fast for Mercy. She's excited about the possibility of seeing her mother. Jesse makes meatloaf for dinner, Mercy has never had meatloaf before and she loves it. But the thought of seeing her mother keeps running through her head.

Mercy goes to bed early so the next day will come faster. She opens the bedroom door and is surprised by her new bed. Destinee gave her the side of the room with the window, since she spent years in a windowless room.

"Destinee, you and your family are so good to me. I appreciate it. I just want to see my mother one time, just once."

"You'll see her tomorrow."

"Thank you."

"Now I'm going to try out my new bed. Good night, Destinee. I mean, good night, Sis."

"Good night, Sis."

The next morning arrives fast for Mercy, she's too excited to sleep.

She's already getting dressed before Jesse knocks on the door to wake them. Destinee wakes and is surprised to see Mercy half-dressed. She knows the reason behind her excitement, the possibility of seeing her mother. Destinee just hopes they can get away with it without anyone finding out. She would hate for Master Kisen to send Mercy back to the reform school.

"Destinee, do you think this is a bad idea? If you do, we don't have to go."

"No. I promised you. We'll make it without getting caught."

Classes drag for Mercy, her eyes constantly on the clock. Finally, school is over. Destinee calls her brother to say they'll be late and not to tell their parents. Then she calls a cab to take them to the bordello, only a 10-minute drive from the school.

It's a huge, magnificent, three-story white building trimmed in gold. A doorman stands at the entrance. They need a plan to get in. Spotting a restaurant across the street, they pick up some food and pretend to make a delivery. It works. The doorman lets them in and tells them to inform the woman at the desk that they have a food delivery.

The woman behind the desk looks them up and down.

"What do you young ladies need?"

Destinee speaks up. "We have a delivery for Claudette Campbell." The woman calls up to Claudette's room.

"What is it? I didn't order anything."

"Maybe one of your clients ordered it for you."

"Have them bring it up."

"Take it up to room 333."

The girls head to the elevator. The door opens slowly, revealing two grungy-looking white men. They step back with their heads down, avoiding eye contact. The elevator smells of alcohol, cigarettes, and worse.

Mercy wrinkles her nose and glances at Destinee.

"It stinks in here." Then, with a disgusted look, she adds softly,

"Just think, I could have ended up here in a couple of years if you hadn't saved me. Thank you."

The elevator opens on the third floor. They walk down the hall, hearing squeaking beds and the moans of men and women. They stop at room 333 and listen at the door to be sure Claudette is alone. The only sound is the television. They knock. A soft voice invites them in.

Destinee opens the door, walking in with Mercy shyly behind her. Claudette is sitting on the couch, watching television without looking up.

"Set it on the dresser. And thank you," she says.

Mercy stares at her, wondering if she'll look up and recognize her. Claudette is a beautiful dark-skinned woman, short, slim, with curly coal-black hair. Mercy actually favors her mother. Claudette never looks up. Mercy glances at Destinee and shrugs, unsure what to do.

Destinee takes matters into her own hands.

"Ms. Claudette, this is Mercy. She's your daughter. She wanted to see you."

"She's my what?"

"She's your daughter."

Claudette gets up and walks over to Mercy. She takes her by the chin, examining her face.

"Mercy… it is you."

She hugs her tightly, kissing her cheeks.

"I thought I'd never see you again."

She tells Mercy she never stopped thinking about her and always wished to see her again. She had asked her Master many times for permission but he refused.

Mercy tells her about life in reform school, how she met Destinee, and how Destinee saved her by asking her Master to buy her so she'd have a better chance at life.

Claudette hugs Destinee and thanks her for saving her daughter from a horrible Master and a doomed future. She tells Mercy how happy she is to see her but doesn't want her to come back. Now she can live her life knowing her daughter is safe and has a bright future.

She kisses Mercy and walks her to the door.

"Remember one thing, Mercy, your father loved you very much, and so do I. Go home, baby."

Destinee and Mercy catch a cab home without saying a word. They just smile at each other. They make it home before their parents and go up to their room.

Chapter 27
The Update

—*m*—

Tonight is Poker Night at James's house, as he calls their meetings.

Gabriel is the first to arrive, so James fills him in on the organization. Nationwide, 223 slaves have escaped to freedom, and 20 have bought theirs.

"The election's looking good. It looks like our man will represent the Democrats. He might win, and if he doesn't, we may be going to war."

James informs Gabriel that the location of the deactivation devices for the chips has been found, and they're going to take control of the country one way or another.

"Gabriel, our network spreads wide. We've been preparing for this for years. We have people in the Senate and Congress. This will take more than one man, we need people behind the President to succeed."

The rest of the men arrive and begin filling Gabriel in on the details of their plans.

Chapter 28
Graduation Day

———⟪⟫———

Hope is in her room getting ready for the graduation ceremony. She's been trying to reach Akim since she returned from Paris with no success. She has no idea Akim saw Kisen drop her off when they returned. She needs to talk to him about ending their relationship. She's fallen in love with Kisen but wants to end things with Akim without hurting him. They've been together since college, but now she realizes she wasn't truly in love. Knowing Kisen has shown her what love really is, she understands it's nothing like what she had with Akim. She hopes to see him at the ceremony and maybe talk then.

There's a knock at her door. Thinking it's Akim, she opens it, but to her surprise, it's Kisen.

"Hey, what are you doing here?"

"I brought you something. I want you to wear it."

He fastens a three-carat diamond pendant on her neck. "Just a little graduation gift."

She looks in the mirror. "Oh my, it's beautiful."

"Not as beautiful as you."

"You've done so much for me already. Remember, I'm a slave in America. You can't keep doing things like this."

"Don't you belong to me? I can do what I want."

"But what will people think?"

"I don't care what they think."

"Come on, you need to go to the auditorium."

"I need to finish getting ready."

He kisses her and leaves. As he's walking down the hall, he passes Akim, who recognizes him. Akim knocks on Hope's door. Thinking it's Kisen again, she opens it.

"What did you forget…" She stops, surprised to see Akim.

"Nope, it's me. I knew something was going on with you and him. I saw him drop you off after your weekend together."

"Akim…"

"Don't deny it. You're in a relationship with your Master, and it doesn't look like you're unwilling, Hope."

"Akim, we need to talk."

"About what? I'm not blind. We had plans, and you threw it away. I came that night to apologize for jumping to conclusions about your Master, but as I said, you're willing."

"Goodbye, Hope."

"But Akim…"

"Goodbye, Hope."

Akim walks out, heartbroken, tears running down his face. Hope stands there, wiping her eyes, feeling confused and torn. She wonders if she truly loves Akim or Kisen. Akim and she had planned to buy their freedom together, but Kisen showed her another kind of freedom. She feels overwhelmed. She looks at the clock; she has to get to the auditorium. She sits on her bed and begins to cry.

Kisen finds a seat at the bottom arena where the slave owners sit to watch their property receive degrees, after all, it increases their income.

Destinee notices Master Kisen below. "Look, Dad, there's Master Kisen." Gabriel is surprised to see him. Most Masters couldn't care less about graduations and just sit at home collecting money, but Master Kisen has proven many times he's different.

The ceremony is short, with only a little over 100 graduates. While waiting for Hope, Kisen makes his way to the lobby to meet the family. Gabriel sees Akim and invites him over to wait for Hope, not knowing they're no longer together. Akim declines, saying they're not together anymore.

Gabriel asks why. Akim glances at Kisen and tells him he'll have to ask Hope, then walks away, passing her without a word. Gabriel notices and asks Hope what's going on.

"Dad, you know we belong to different plantations. Now that we've graduated, we won't be able to see each other, so we decided to end it."

"We'll talk about it later."

"OK, Dad. Later."

"Congratulations, Hope." Hope turns and sees Kisen.

"Thank you, sir."

"Why do you look so sad? You just graduated at the top of your class."

"I know, sir. I'm just tired. I'll be alright."

"I have to set you up at the hospital with your mother so you can get started."

"Thank you."

"Do you want your own place, or do you still plan to live with your parents?"

"I guess I'll need my own place, sir."

"Then we need to start looking."

Master Kisen can tell Hope is hiding something. He wonders what's happened since he last saw her before the graduation ceremony, something must have.

Destinee and Mercy slowly walk up to him.

"Well hello, Destinee. Are you and Mercy being good?"

"Yes, sir. We are. And Mercy's doing really well in school."

"Good. Glad to hear that."

Kisen calls Hope to the side. "Come here, Hope. I need to talk to you."

"Yes, sir."

"I need to see you again. We have to make some time before you start working."

"Back to Paris?" she asks with a smile.

He laughs. "No, we've got too much to do. I need to find you a place, somewhere you won't feel uncomfortable with me visiting, and get you set up at the hospital."

Hope is distracted by Akim standing in the distance, watching them. He starts to approach.

"Do your parents know?" he asks.

"Know what?"

"About you and your Master."

Kisen hears him and grabs Akim. "Have you forgotten your place?" he asks.

"No, sir." Akim backs away and walks off.

Gabriel goes after him. "What is going on with you and Hope?"

"Ask your daughter."

Gabriel looks back at Hope and Master Kisen. That's his Master. He knows his place and that he isn't allowed to question him, but he will continue this with Hope when they get home.

Master Kisen congratulates Hope and tells her goodbye.

"Goodbye, Kisen…" She suddenly realizes what she said.

"I mean, goodbye, Master Kisen."

But it's too late. Everyone heard, and saw that he didn't react, as if it were normal.

Master Kisen leaves, and Gabriel looks at Hope. "We're going to have a little talk when we get home. I want to know what's going on."

When they arrive at the house, Gabriel tells the kids to go upstairs so they can talk to Hope.

"I don't want to put a damper on graduation day, this is a day of new beginnings for you, but you need to explain to me and your mother what's going on."

"I told you, Dad. We decided to end it. We're from two different plantations, how can we continue our relationship?"

"He doesn't seem happy about it. And what does Master have to do with this?"

"Nothing, Dad. Master Kisen came to the University to see me one day and Akim saw him. I guess he was jealous."

"Why would he be jealous of your Master? He's your Master."

Jesse asks, "Is there a reason he should feel that way?"

"No, Mom."

"Why did Master come to see you?" asks Jesse.

"He brought me a graduation gift."

"A gift? Why would he do that? Masters don't give gifts."

"Mom, hasn't he proved he's different from his father? Hasn't he been doing a lot of things Masters don't usually do?"

"Well, I hope he's not doing you."

As soon as those words leave Jesse's mouth, she notices the diamond necklace peeking from under Hope's blouse. She walks up and pulls it out.

"Wow. Is this what he gave you? It must be. You can't afford something like this, you don't own any jewelry."

"He gave it to me."

"This is very expensive, Hope. Why would he buy you something so expensive?"

Hope's father speaks up. "I have a question, Hope."

"Yes, sir?"

"You called him Kisen, and I could tell you were comfortable saying his name. It didn't even bother him. How could you get away with something so disrespectful?"

"I don't know, Dad."

"You and your sister have lost your minds. He is our Master. Don't forget that."

"Yes, Dad."

"Is there anything else you need to tell us?" asks Jesse.

"No, ma'am."

Upstairs, the kids have their doors cracked, listening to the conversation. Destinee whispers to Mercy, "I told you we have a good Master."

Mercy nods in agreement as they close the door softly and start to giggle.

Chapter 29
Anthony Hamilton

—◊◊◊—

Gabriel arrives at James's house for another meeting. James explains that their victory is guaranteed by the population of free Blacks and the white population who believe their candidate is white.

"When he gets in office, that's when the real work begins."

Gabriel asks why Anthony was chosen to run for the presidency.

James tells him to take a seat so he can explain Anthony Hamilton's story and why he was selected to represent them.

Anthony's father came from a political family of mayors, senators, and governors. He himself was a governor. Their family also owned one of the largest plantations in the South. Anthony's mother was a slave, the daughter of the family's head housemaid. Because her mother ran the house slaves, they lived in the main house.

The plantation was very large, with many children. Anthony's grandfather had even built a school on the property for slave children, hiring the best teachers to ensure quality education. Since the school was on his land, he didn't have to follow segregation laws, all the children, both white and enslaved, attended together. Friendships developed, including between Anthony's parents.

Anthony's mother worked in the house with her mother, so she and his father grew up around each other. Friendship turned to love, but they kept it hidden, interracial relationships were frowned upon, and he knew his family would never approve.

It was easy enough to conceal. They would escape to the west wing of the house, unused unless there were overnight guests. They managed to hide their relationship for about a year and a half, until Anthony's mother became pregnant. She tried to hide it as long as possible, but everyone knew that a child born to a slave would also be considered a slave, no matter the father. They had seen it happen many times.

Her mother noticed the weight gain and pressed her until she confessed. When she learned the father was the Master's son, she was furious and terrified. She cried, fearing her daughter and the baby would be sold. She begged her daughter not to reveal the father, saying they would blame a slave boy instead.

Anthony's father stayed quiet, too, afraid of what his own father might do. He loved her, but feared she and the child would be sold away.

Mistress Hamilton eventually noticed the pregnancy and asked the girl's mother who the father was, since they would need to record it in the database. Caught off guard, she stalled, but knew the truth would come out. A DNA test of all slaves was routine to prevent inbreeding, and it would reveal the father.

That night, after dinner, Anthony's father told his parents the truth: the child was his, and he loved her. His parents were upset, but they loved their son. His father laughed, saying this wasn't the first time something like this had happened, nor would it be the last. What was unusual, however, was their son falling in love with a slave.

Anthony's mother took the news harder. She reminded her son he was only eighteen and didn't know what love was. She told his father to sell the girl and baby, he would get over it. But Anthony insisted he loved her and begged not to be separated. His father, loving his son and wanting him happy, told his wife their son was nearly a man now and must make his own decisions.

He allowed them to stay, but under one condition: no one could ever know Anthony was the father. They all agreed, at least for now.

Two months later, Anthony's mother went into labor. Because she was Black, she had to go to the hospital for Blacks. She reported it to Master Hamilton, and he made the arrangements.

As she was taken into the delivery room, Anthony's father walked in, to everyone's surprise, especially since his own father was with him. With his arm around his son, he said, "I can't miss the birth of my first grandchild."

It was a hard delivery, and Anthony's mother died during childbirth. The nurse handed the baby to his father. The child was so light-skinned he could pass as white, and the family decided that's how he would be raised, for his protection and theirs.

His father and grandfather adored him. His grandmother took longer to accept him but eventually grew to love him. She became his nanny, caring for him daily, but was forbidden to tell him who she really was.

He often asked about his mother and why there were no pictures of her. It broke her heart every time. She kept a photo hidden in her room, hoping one day the truth would be told.

That day finally came when Anthony turned twenty-one. That's when his father and grandfather decided to tell him the truth. They also brought in the woman he knew as his nanny and told him she was really his grandmother. He took the news surprisingly well. His family were good people, who treated their slaves kindly, so Anthony was raised in a loving household. His grandmother, who had cared for him, made sure he understood his black heritage, even though he hadn't known he was a part of it. He loved her and the others as family. He grew up understanding the world he lived in and the role he was meant to play.

Anthony traveled the world with his father, saw blacks living as free men, and wanted the same for his country. His father, following in his own father's footsteps, became a governor. Without realizing it, Anthony was being prepared for politics.

"You see, Gabriel, Anthony and I grew up together as friends. When he shared his story with me, I shared with him my world of the Underground. Together we came up with the idea of him running for President. With his family's political background, he has the best chance of winning."

Around the room, some members already knew the story while others did not. James saw Anthony, walked up to him, and shook his hand.

"Thank you, Mr. Hamilton, for all that you have done, and all that you are about to do."

Chapter 30
The Brothel

—◦◦◦—

While everyone was caught up in their own lives, Destinee and Mercy had been visiting Claudette at the brothel. Everyone there had grown used to seeing the girls and even enjoyed their visits. But on this day, Samuel decided to follow them.

The girls had found a shortcut they now used, and they never told Samuel where they went after school, worried he'd tell their parents. But Samuel was curious. He knew what a brothel was, he'd heard the boys at school talk about it. That's where Masters sent female slaves who weren't considered useful for anything else. He'd even heard someone say Mercy could have ended up there if his family hadn't taken her in. So why were the girls going inside?

Samuel waited outside until a police officer noticed him.

"What are you doing here?" the officer asked.

"I'm waiting for my sister."

"Where is she?"

"She's in there," Samuel said, pointing at the brothel.

"Why?"

"I don't know."

The officer put him in the back of the car and entered his name into the database to locate his Master.

Moments later, Destinee and Mercy came out, not noticing Samuel behind the glass.

"There's my sister, right there," Samuel told the officer.

The officer called the girls over. They approached, confused, until they saw Samuel sitting inside.

"Samuel, what are you doing here?" Destinee asked.

He hung his head and stayed silent.

The officer asked why the girls were in a brothel. Mercy spoke up:

"Visiting my mother."

He then asked if they'd left Samuel outside. They said they hadn't known he followed them. The officer told them to get in the back of the car.

Destinee turned to Samuel. "Why'd you follow us?"

"Wanted to see why I keep covering for you."

"You haven't covered for us. We get home before Mom and Dad, so you've never had to."

"Now you got us all in trouble."

"You got yourselves in trouble."

Mercy began to cry. "Master Kisen's going to send me back."

"Don't worry," Samuel muttered.

"Where's he taking us?" he asked.

Mercy looked out the window. "To Master Kisen."

When the car pulled up, Master Kisen was already sitting on the porch waiting. The officer released the children and explained where he had found them. Kisen sent them onto the porch while he finished speaking with the officer. The three sat with heads down, more ashamed than afraid, except Mercy, who was terrified of being sent back to the reform school.

When Kisen finally joined them, he sat down and studied their faces in silence. The girls began to cry.

"Why are you crying?" he asked.

Mercy whispered, "Are you going to send me back to reform school?"

"Should I? You too, Destinee?"

"No, sir," Destinee said quickly.

"Why were you girls at a brothel? Let me guess, you went to see your mother."

"Yes, sir."

Mercy explained that she and Destinee had been visiting after school but always made it home before their parents. She told him it wasn't Destinee's fault, she just wanted to know her mother.

"OK, now you know her, what now?"

"I don't know, sir."

"I'll tell you what: it stops now. Don't come back here. If I sell you back to your old Master, you'll spend plenty of time here with your mother. Is that what you want?"

"No, sir. Please don't send me back."

"I gave you a chance for a better life. Don't throw it away."

"And you, Destinee, what were you thinking? Why didn't you try to talk her out of it instead of going along with her?"

"I just wanted her to know her mother."

"I'm taking you back so you can say one final goodbye, but this is the last time. Do you understand?"

"Yes, sir," the girls replied.

The drive back was silent. Mercy loved visiting her mother, but she had to obey Master Kisen or risk everything for herself and Destinee. Destinee's mind was on her parents, dreading what they'd say if they found out. She also felt bad for Mercy, who had enjoyed her mother's company so much. Samuel, who had never cared much for Mercy being around, thinking she was a replacement for his brother, now felt guilty. If he hadn't followed them, none of this would have happened.

At the brothel, Master Kisen told the woman at the desk they were there to see Claudette. She recognized Mercy and called Claudette, saying she had guests. As they left for the elevator, she called again to add, "Mercy's here with her Master."

Claudette wrapped herself in a robe, straightened her room, and answered the knock. She let them in. Kisen explained he was bringing Mercy to say her last goodbye. Mother and daughter hugged, both crying. Claudette told Kisen she understood, this wasn't a place for her daughter. She admitted she was only selfish because seeing Mercy brought her joy.

"Mercy, the time I've shared with you has been the best of my life. I'm so glad you found me. Take care of yourself, my sweet girl. But he's right, you can't come back."

"I promise I won't, but I'll never forget you, Momma. I love you. I'll be good, I'll do well in school, I'll get a job and save my money, and I'll buy you, I promise."

Claudette smiled sadly. "Sweetheart, a slave can't buy a slave."

Mercy burst into tears. "Then I'll give my money to Master Kisen to buy you."

Kisen watched the exchange, moved despite himself. "Come on, Mercy. It's time to go."

Mercy hugged her mother again, then followed him out. The drive home was quiet except for Mercy's sniffles. When they arrived, no cars were in the drive; their parents weren't home yet. Kisen told them they could share the truth if they wanted; he wasn't going to say anything. As they got out, Mercy lingered.

"Thank you," she whispered.

"I don't want you going back there, Mercy. But I'll see what I can do so you can see your mother."

"Really?"

"Like I said, I'll see what I can do."

"Thank you, sir."

"Now go inside. I'll wait out here for Hope."

Mercy entered to find Destinee and Samuel waiting.

"What did he say?" Samuel asked.

"He said he'll see what he can do so I can see my mother again," Mercy replied with a smile.

"I told you he was nice," Destinee said.

Samuel glanced out the window. "If he's not going to say anything, then why's he still out there?"

"He's waiting for Hope," Mercy answered.

"Why?"

"I think he likes her," Destinee said.

"I think she likes him too," Mercy added.

As Samuel started up the stairs, he stopped and turned. "I think he likes all of us."

Chapter 31
Hopes Condo

———

Jesse and Hope pulled into the driveway and got out of the car. Jesse approached Master Kisen.

"I need to talk to Hope, Jesse," Kisen said.

"Yes, sir."

Hope walked up to him. "Sir, can I help you?" she said with a wink.

"Get in the car. I need to talk to you."

Hope climbed into the back seat.

"Dammit, I forgot to drive the truck."

Kisen turned to her. "I want you up here."

"Kisen, your windows aren't tinted. You know I can't ride in the front with you."

"I'm going to tint all my vehicles so I don't have to deal with this."

He started driving off.

"Where are we going?" Hope asked.

"First, I'm taking this car back to get my truck so you can sit up here with me."

They drove to the plantation, switched into Kisen's black truck with tinted windows, especially for her.

"This is much better," he said, kissing her.

"Now where are we going?"

"You know you're not supposed to ask me questions."

"I'm sorry. I guess I'm getting too comfortable with you."

"Baby, you know I'm kidding. You can ask me anything. I'm taking you to see your new place."

"I have a place?"

"No, you have a condo. I hope you like it."

"I'm sure I will."

"I wanted you on the plantation so you could be close to me, but I knew tongues would wag. I don't really care, I just don't want you uncomfortable. The place I got for you is more private."

"Is it close to the bus or train station so I can get to work? I won't be riding with my mother."

"You'll be fine. I'm taking care of that too."

Kisen stopped in front of a gate to a multi-level garage, drove inside, and parked. He smiled at Hope. "Here we are."

He took her hand. She quickly pulled away. "Have you forgotten where we are?"

"I don't give a damn," he said, grabbing her hand again.

They walked to the elevator. The door opened on the 30th floor, which had only two condos, one on each side of the building. Kisen opened the door to Hope's condo. She stepped in slowly, shocked. White marble floors, white walls, tall ceilings, black leather furniture with glass accent tables, a matching glass dinette set, a black-and-glass bar in the corner, huge windows reaching the ceiling, and a patio door opening onto a big terrace.

"Oh my, Kisen, this is beautiful."

She walked into the bedroom and found a huge black king-size bed with white satin bedding. Another large patio door led out to a balcony overlooking the city. "This reminds me of Paris, without the Eiffel Tower."

"I know. That's why I got it for you. You loved that patio overlooking Paris, everything except the tower."

"I love it, but it's too much. What will my parents think? They'll know it would take three lifetimes to afford a place like this. No, a slave could never afford a place like this."

"Then tell them the truth, that we're together and love each other."

"Hope, you're mine. I don't have to explain anything to anyone, not even your parents."

"I know," she said, worried.

"You have everything here you'll need."

"Kisen, you're spoiling me."

"I know, and I love it."

"Everyone will find out."

"What did I just say? I don't care. You're mine."

He pulled her close and kissed her passionately. He picked her up, carried her to the bed, and they made passionate love all night, talking about their adventures in Paris, free to show their love in public.

"I miss that life, Kisen."

"So do I. Maybe we'll move there and get married."

"Stop playing."

"Who's playing?"

Kisen told Hope to hold on, he needed to make a phone call. "Hello, this is Kisen Brown, Hope's owner. I'm calling to tell you she won't be there tomorrow."

He hung up.

"Why did you do that?"

"Because you're spending the day with me, breaking this place in."

"But…"

"But nothing. You heard what I said." He kissed her again.

"This doesn't feel real. Before I can adjust to one surprise, you come with another."

"Are you complaining?"

"No, Kisen, I'm just trying to mentally adjust. I'm happy, excited, and afraid."

"Afraid of what?"

"I don't know. I don't know where this is going to end up."

"Stop worrying. You have nothing to worry about, unless you're worried about me. Are you?"

She looked up at him, afraid to admit she feared he might be playing with her and would throw her away when he was done.

"Hope, you have nothing to worry about. I won't let anything happen to you. And if you're worried about me, don't. I love you."

Morning comes too fast for Hope. She wakes up and opens the patio blinds.

"Oh, Kisen, what have you done?"

Hope finds a painting of the Eiffel Tower on the patio door that Kisen painted after she fell asleep.

She finds him still asleep and kisses him until he wakes.

"What are you smiling about, woman?"

"You're so good to me."

"What did I do?"

"You know what you did, the painting of the Eiffel Tower on the patio door."

"You like that?"

"I loved it. You're so talented."

"Couldn't let Akim outdo me."

"No one could outdo you."

Kisen jumps out of bed and walks onto the patio.

"Kisen Brown, I love you."

"And I love you, Hope Brown."

She can't believe how her life has changed, she's wondering where it's going. She's in love with her Master, and he loves her. They walk out onto the patio and look down at the hustle and bustle of the city, watching the brown-skinned people heading to work.

"Hey, babe, you look like you're in deep thought. You alright?"

"Yes, I'm good, just thinking about how happy I am."

"Babe, I need your advice about something."

Kisen tells Hope about the situation with Mercy and her mother. He asks Hope what he should do, if anything.

Hope's suggestion is to buy her, she won't cost much since her classification is low.

"But what could she do? She's been working as a hooker. What other skills could she have for me to regain my losses?"

"Ask her. I'm sure there's something valuable she can do, or she can be trained."

"It's not like buying a child and training them, she's a grown woman."

"She can live on the plantation and work as a cook or a maid. Why are you trying to help?"

"I feel bad for Mercy. She wants to get to know her mother and spend time with her. But they didn't have any business visiting her at the bordello."

"Yes, you're right."

"I'll think about it."

Chapter 32
Election Day

———

Election Day is finally here. This is what the Underground has been working so hard for. The race is very close, almost neck-and-neck. James is nervous, he didn't think it would be this close. He wonders if all this was for nothing. Even if he gets into the White House, there will still be a lot of work ahead. He'll need a House majority to abolish slavery. First things first, they have to win.

The day is long. Gabriel has a hard time concentrating at work, worried about the election. His drive home feels endless, traffic jammed because of the voting polls. He finally reaches home, lies on the couch, and watches the news. It's still close. He's never cared about presidential elections before, why would it matter who became President? They were still slaves. But this time it's different. This could mean freedom. This could change everything.

Gabriel tries to understand the electoral votes, it doesn't make sense to him. Popular votes should be what counts. He's trying to keep his eyes open, but exhaustion takes over and he falls asleep. After about an hour, the phone rings, jolting him awake. He knocks it to the floor, grabs it, and hangs it up. "Oh my God, it was James." He calls him back.

"We won, we won!"

"We won?" Gabriel shouts.

He turns the TV up. They're announcing the newly elected President, Anthony Hamilton. Gabriel and James finish their conversation, overjoyed. Gabriel hears Jesse in the kitchen and runs to tell her the good news.

"We have a black president! We're going to be free!"

Jesse puts her hand over his mouth. "Be quiet before the kids hear you. Isn't this supposed to be a secret?"

"Yes, it is. I'm sorry. I just got excited," he laughs.

"We still have a way to go."

"I know. But we're on our way, babe. Freedom is just over the horizon, and we're going to be alive to see it."

They hear the front door open, it's Hope.

"You know you can't tell her. You weren't supposed to tell me," Jesse says.

"I know."

Hope walks in and sees the newscast about the election.

"Why are you watching that mess? You know it has nothing to do with us. They only care about white people. It's not like the new president is going to set us free." She turns off the TV.

"Where have you been?" asks Gabriel.

"Master Kisen found me an apartment. I've been staying there and getting it together."

"He's awfully attentive when it comes to you."

"Oh, Mom, stop it."

"What about the car you just pulled up in?"

"Since I'm living on my own, he felt I needed a car."

"He bought you a car too? What the hell is going on with you two? Masters don't buy their slaves cars. Slaves ride the bus and trains until they can afford to buy one."

"Mom, I have to go upstairs and pack some of my things."

Hope runs upstairs.

"Jesse, if something is going on, there's nothing we can do about it. He owns her. She belongs more to him than to us. Stop asking her, forcing her to lie to us. She's probably ashamed."

"Don't worry, Jesse. We're on our way to freedom, remember that. Our kids will be free, free to do what they want, with whomever they want. So don't worry."

"Okay, I'll stop. It will eventually come out. Whatever goes on in the dark will come to light."

Hope is packing her things and suddenly feels sick. She runs to the bathroom and just makes it. She wonders what made her sick, maybe something she ate. She shakes it off and goes back to packing.

The kids hear Hope packing and come into her room. They hug her goodbye. She tells them she'll visit often and even take them to see her apartment, then remembers how elaborate it is and wonders how she'll explain it.

She goes downstairs where her parents are waiting and hugs them goodbye.

"When can we come and see your new place?" her mother asks.

"As soon as I get it together," Hope replies, thinking, How am I going to get away with this? She knows her apartment is far too nice for a slave girl fresh out of college.

Hope walks out the door and into her new life with her Master.

Chapter 33
A New Addition

—✶—

Two months go by. Hope has been continuously getting sick and doesn't know why she can't keep food down. Kisen grows worried and decides to take her to the plantation doctor. He waits in the lobby while she goes back.

The nurse takes a urine sample, and the doctor examines her. After getting the results, Master Kisen is called back.

"It appears she's pregnant, eight weeks," the doctor says.

"I'll write a prescription for prenatal vitamins."

Kisen doesn't say a word, and neither does Hope. They're both in shock. They'd been using precautions.

In the car, on the way back to the apartment, Kisen finally speaks.

"You had the implant, didn't you?"

"Yes. I don't know why it didn't work."

He says nothing more. It's obvious he's not happy about the news. When they pull up to the apartment, Hope asks, "You're not coming up?"

"No. I have things to do at the plantation."

Hope goes up alone for the first time since she moved in. She throws herself on the bed and starts to cry. She's heard stories of Masters getting their slaves pregnant, then abandoning them or selling the babies. She thought Kisen was different, that he truly loved her. How could she have been so wrong? How could he leave her at a time like this?

She's scared and has no one to talk to. She wants to call her mother but hesitates. Finally, she picks up the phone.

"Mama, can you come over? I need you, please."

She cries again, gives her mother the address, and hangs up. Quickly she hides all traces of Kisen before her mother arrives. The last thing on her mind is how to explain the apartment, but she knows it will be hard.

Kisen arrives back at his house, angry, angry at himself for not being more careful. He was caught up in the moment, living it up in Paris with Hope. It was beautiful. He does love her, but he's not ready for a baby, especially in the world they live in.

Suddenly, an alarm sounds: a slave is traveling without permission. He checks the monitor, it's Jesse, heading toward Hope's apartment. He could intervene, but he won't. Hope needs her.

Kisen starts to feel bad. He shouldn't have left Hope alone. He decides to go back after her mother leaves. They need to talk. After all, this isn't her fault, it's his.

Jesse arrives at the condos, shocked at how Hope could afford such a place. She presses the buzzer. Hope sees her on the camera and sends the elevator down. She's already standing at the door when her mother arrives. They hug, and Hope begins to cry.

"What's wrong, Hope? What's going on, baby?"

"Mom, I'm pregnant."

"By who?" her mother asks.

"Mom, I can't tell you."

"Why not, Hope? Is it Akim?"

"No, Mother. It's not Akim."

"Is it Master Kisen? Is that why he's so attentive?" she says with a smirk.

"Mom…"

"What's going on with you? And this place, you can't afford this." Jesse starts walking around the condo.

"This is definitely out of your range. Your father and I together couldn't afford this, so how can you?" She opens the closet, admiring Hope's clothes.

"All these colorful clothes, you can't even wear these. Why do you have all this? Where did it come from? What's going on here?"

While looking through the closet, Jesse finds a pair of men's pants Hope overlooked.

"Who do these belong to?"

"Mom, please, I need you here for me. You'll know everything, but not now, please."

"Baby, tell the truth. I know it's either Akim or Master Kisen. But I'd bet on Master Kisen. You couldn't live like this unless it's him. Plus, you belong to him. You must think I'm stupid."

"I promise, you will know everything."

"I already know everything."

"Why did you call me over, Hope? I thought you wanted to tell me what's going on."

"I do, Mom, but this isn't the right time."

"This is definitely the right time. Did he leave when he found out you were pregnant?"

"Mom, I just want you to hold me and tell me everything's going to be alright. Mama, please."

"Come here, baby. I can do that."

Jesse leads Hope to the couch, sits, and holds her daughter in her arms.

"Baby, you're the smartest woman I know. I know you're going to make the right decisions about whatever you're doing."

"Thank you, Mama. I love you."

"But you've got to stop keeping secrets from me and your dad."

"I'll tell you everything. I promise, Mama."

"I better get home. I didn't ask permission from Master Kisen. I know he sees my location, that's why I haven't heard from him."

"I'll see you in the morning at work, Mama."

Jesse kisses her daughter and takes the elevator.

Hope goes to bed wishing Kisen were there. It's her first night sleeping alone since she's been with him. She wonders when she'll see him again, or if she will. She can't believe she could have been wrong about him. She cries herself to sleep, dreading work in the morning.

Kisen is parked in the garage, waiting for Jesse to leave. He watches her drive away, then sits in his car, wondering what to say to Hope. He knows he shouldn't have left her alone, she needed him.

He opens the door quietly, not wanting to wake her if she's asleep. He finds her lying on the bed, still in her clothes. He lays down beside her and kisses her cheek. She slowly opens her eyes, not saying a word, overjoyed he came back. He pulls her into his arms and whispers, "I'm sorry I left you alone. I needed to think."

She doesn't reply. They both fall asleep.

Chapter 34
Christmas

—◦◦◦—

A month passes, and preparations are underway for Christmas in the Brown household. Christmas Eve has always been spent on the plantation, a tradition the Masters have followed for generations.

The slaves are given three days off work and allowed to keep their entire paycheck instead of handing over their share. All are required to gather together on Christmas Eve to party, eat, and celebrate.

This year is bittersweet for Gabriel's family, the first Christmas without their son, but the first with Mercy, who has never experienced a real Christmas. The family goes all out to make it special, showing her what Christmas is meant to be. They've grown to love her as one of their own.

Mercy misses her mother, especially after spending time with her at the brothel, but since Master Kisen forbade them from visiting, they haven't been back. She's happy with her new family and grateful for the life they've given her. She won't disobey Kisen.

The family rides to the plantation, Hope included. It will be the first time she and Kisen spend the night apart, but he refuses to break tradition by skipping Christmas at the plantation with his family. He hasn't spent much time there since being with Hope.

Gabriel drives through the gates, beautifully decorated with huge wreaths. The trees are strung with white lights. They pass Master Brown's house, then Kisen's siblings' homes, before reaching Kisen's house, where he sits on the porch with his father and siblings. Hope longs to be with him but knows she can't, not yet. Maybe one day.

They arrive at the celebration. Gabriel spots his parents, siblings, and extended family, he hasn't seen them since his son's funeral. Jesse takes Mercy over for introductions, then to meet her side of the family.

There are only four holidays when Masters allow families to gather freely: New Year's Eve, Easter, Thanksgiving, and Christmas.

Everyone enjoys the celebration, especially Mercy. She never imagined anything like this. Life outside the reform school is better than she ever dreamed. She's even happier when she sees a Santa Claus passing out gifts. To her surprise, she gets one, her first Christmas gift. She doesn't want to open it yet. She wants to take it home, put it under the tree, and open it Christmas morning.

Just when the night couldn't get better, Master Kisen walks in with a beautiful Black woman. Hope notices her first, wondering who she is and why she's with Kisen. Then Mercy lets out a squeal:

"It's Mama!"

As Kisen brings her to the table, Mercy runs into her arms.

"Merry Christmas, Mercy," he says.

Mercy wants to hug him too, but she holds back. Even though she's seen Hope do it, she can't bring herself to, though she knows he wouldn't mind.

"Thank you so much, Master Kisen. This is the best Christmas I could have dreamed of."

He smiles and turns to walk away, hearing her tell her mother, "I wish we could keep you forever."

"I'm working on it. Ask your mom," Kisen replies.

"What is it, Mom? What does he mean?"

"I'll tell you later, sweetie."

Mercy introduces her mother to the family, and together they spend the evening dancing, eating, and exchanging gifts, a Christmas like no other.

As the evening comes to an end, Master Kisen slips back in and sits beside Hope.

"That was a wonderful thing you did for Mercy, she's so happy."

"She's had a hard life. She kept her promise not to go back to the bordello, she's doing well in school, keeping her grades up. I wanted to do something special for her and make her first Christmas memorable."

"And you did. Did you buy her mother?"

"Yes. Your family is really costing me," he laughs.

"What responsibility will she have?"

"I don't know yet. We threw some ideas around. She said she used to do the women's hair at the bordello for extra money."

"That's a good idea, I can help her get started."

"Be my guest. I'll give her six months, then I'll start collecting my share."

"Kisen, you're a good man. You don't treat slaves badly like the rest of your family. If I can speak freely, it's like you don't even share the same blood."

"Come on, babe. Let's dance."

"You know we can't dance together."

"Why not? Don't you belong to me? Isn't this my plantation?"

"Yes, but…"

Before she could finish, Kisen takes her hand and pulls her onto the floor. They begin a slow dance. He places her hands around his neck, then wraps his arms around her waist and pulls her close. She nervously glances at her parents, then around the room. Everyone has stopped to watch. She whispers in his ear, "Everyone is staring. Why did you do this?"

"Because I can, and because I wanted to. Hope, look at me. Just imagine we're back in Paris, dancing."

She looks into his eyes and immediately feels better.

"In a few months, everyone will know anyway. Have you told your parents about us, that I'm the father?"

"No. Not yet. My mother knows I'm pregnant, but not who the father is. She suspects it's you."

"Do you want to tell them together, or alone?"

"Together. But not yet."

The song ends, and Kisen motions for Claudette to leave. Claudette hugs Mercy and tells her she'll see her soon.

During the drive home, Mercy tells them about Kisen's plan to let her mother open a shop on the plantation to do hair. Then she asks something she'd never thought of:

"Does this mean you'll leave us and live with your mother?"

"I never thought about that. But I don't want to leave you, you're my sister, and I love you. I love all of you."

Gabriel speaks up. "I guess that settles it. You're staying with us. But you can visit your mother whenever you want."

As they walk into the house, Jesse tells the kids to go upstairs and get ready for bed. "Christmas morning will be here soon."

Hope is about to head upstairs when her mother stops her.

"Hope, wait. We need to talk. Why don't you admit what's going on with you and Master Kisen?"

"I told you, Mom, we've become friends."

"Friends? What's wrong with you, Destinee, and Mercy?" Jesse yells.

"He's not your friend, he's your Master. He owns you. Damn, I'm so sick of hearing this 'friend' nonsense."

"Mother, you know he's better than his father. Things have gotten better, and look what he's done for our family."

"She's right, Jesse. Things are better under him," Gabriel says.

"But is he doing this just because of Hope? Are we the only family he's helping?"

"I don't think so. All the slaves are happier since Master Kisen took charge."

"But stop calling him a friend. He's our Master. If he's such a friend, then let him set us free."

"What about the dance, Hope?"

"He asked me to dance, what was I supposed to say, no?"

"I guess not. Go on to bed, I'm tired."

Jesse and Gabriel finish the night sitting on the couch, staring at the Christmas tree, thinking about their son Seth.

"I wish he was here too, babe," Gabriel says, hugging Jesse.

Christmas morning arrives. Everyone is still in bed after the Christmas Eve celebration, though it's harder this year without Seth.

The first to rise is Mercy. She could hardly sleep from the excitement of her first real Christmas. She wakes Destinee and they head to Samuel's room, but he's already awake. He's sad, it doesn't feel like Christmas without his brother, but he gets up anyway.

The girls jump on Hope's bed. "Come on, let's get Mom and Dad up!"

Everyone goes downstairs to exchange gifts, though Seth's absence is felt by all. Still, they hold it together for Mercy.

They begin with Mercy's gifts. The first is from "Santa Claus," given to her last night at the party. She opens it to find a silver locket. When she opens it, she gasps and begins to cry.

"What's wrong? What is it?" Destinee asks.

"It's a picture of my mother and father."

"I can't believe he did that."

"Who?" Destinee asks.

"You know Master Kisen did it."

There's a knock at the door. Destinee answers, it's Master Kisen and Claudette. He brought her to spend Christmas with her daughter, a surprise Jesse had planned.

Mercy walks up to Kisen. "Thank you."

"For what?"

She opens the locket and shows him the pictures inside. "For this."

"That's from Santa."

"Thank you, Santa," she says with a smile.

She runs to her mother and shows her the pictures. Both are overcome with joy at the gift. Everyone who witnesses it is again amazed by Master Kisen's kindness.

Hope smiles at Kisen, and he smiles back with a wink. Jesse notices the exchange. She knows something is going on between them, especially after that dance last night. She also suspects he's the father, he's the only one always around Hope.

Her thoughts are interrupted when Master Kisen leaves, telling Claudette he'll be back later to pick her up.

Kisen decides to visit his brother and sister for the holidays. He hasn't spent much time with them since most of his spare hours have gone to Hope. At the door, the butler greets him.

"Come in, sir. Master Cruse and Mistress Kiya are in the den."

"Merry Christmas, fam."

"Merry Christmas, big brother," Cruse says.

"Where've you been? We don't see much of you anymore."

"I'm working."

"Hope so, since Dad left you in charge."

"You still mad about that? You kept screwing things up, mistreating slaves, mishandling money. Somebody had to take over. You staying out of trouble, little brother, or do I need to keep an eye on you?"

"What do you care what I'm doing? You've been busy with other things, like Hope."

"Don't start. It's Christmas. I just came to visit my family. Be nice."

"I've been hearing talk around the plantation about you and your slave girl, Hope," Cruse says.

"Haven't you heard it too, sis?"

"Yes, Kisen, I've heard it," Kiya answers.

"Why are you two asking me about something you've both done? And you, sis, didn't you fall in love with your husband's slave?"

"And we've heard you've done the same," Kiya says.

"Have you fallen for this girl?"

"What I do with mine is my business, not yours."

Cruse grabs Kisen's arm. "You'd better be careful before you have a little picaninny running around with black skin and your face."

"If I do, it's my business."

"Anything to say, sis?" Kisen asks.

"Nope."

"You two did your dirt right in Dad's face. You, sis, ruined your marriage because you fell in love with your husband's slave and got pregnant by him. And you, little brother, hunting Dad's slaves like animals and even killing one. So don't tell me what I do is worse."

Cruse pokes Kisen in the chest. "You're no better than us, brother."

"I just stopped by to wish you a Merry Christmas and drop off gifts, not for you to pry into my business."

"Alright, big brother. It's your business. But be careful."

Chapter 35
The kids

—◦◦◦—

Mercy's mom was assigned a house on the plantation with a salon in the back. She's been doing well for herself, saving money. Master Kisen gave her six months before she had to start giving him his share, three months from now. Destinee and Mercy have been working in the shop after school. They taught themselves how to do nails and enjoy making a little money, which Master Kisen allows them to keep. He's proud of them, straight-A students who have such a positive effect on each other. He calls them his little entrepreneurs and tells them to make as much money as they can, because when they come of age, they'll have to start giving him his share.

Samuel is doing better too. Master Kisen suggested therapy to help with the loss of his brother, and it has helped. He's beginning to adjust, though it's been a rough journey.

Hope's pregnancy is clearly showing after seven months, but she still hasn't revealed the father's identity. She'll have to when the baby is born, it's the law, or the hospital will identify him by DNA.

She's both excited and afraid, uncertain of her future. She and Kisen don't spend as much time together as they did at the start of their relationship. She's working, while he's busy with the plantation, the office, and frequent business trips. He stepped up after his brother and sister complained he wasn't taking care of his responsibilities.

Hope worries Kisen won't be there for her, even though he calls regularly to reassure her that she's in his heart, even if he's not physically present. She remembers the stories about Kisen's father getting slave girls pregnant and then selling them. She's even heard the rumor about Kisen's sister Kiya having a child with her husband's slave.

Chapter 36
Kiya

———✦———

Kiya's husband was always away on business trips, leaving her alone. Her slaves catered to her every need. She didn't have many friends, it was just her and them. All she had to do was press the bell and they would appear.

One night, feeling stiff from sitting around, she decided she needed a massage. She told her aid to find a masseuse. The aid reminded her that her husband had one on the plantation and suggested using him. She called him to come and serve his master's wife right away.

The masseuse arrived. The aid opened the door and let him in. He set up his table and invited her over. Kiya looked at him for the first time, and to her surprise, he was beautiful, the most beautiful man she had ever seen. His dark skin gleamed against his white linen shirt and trousers. He was muscular, with smooth features, hazel eyes, perfect white teeth, a bald head that made his features stand out, and a smile that lit up the room.

"Are you ready, ma'am?" he asked, head bowed.

She smiled, though he couldn't see it. He wasn't allowed to look her in the eyes, but she found herself smiling anyway, something she had never done with a slave. The aid noticed the change in her mistress.

That was the start of their relationship. What began with a late-night massage turned into much more. He tried to resist, but as a slave, he couldn't. He feared both her reaction and her husband's if he refused. This continued for several months until she discovered she was pregnant. She knew it couldn't be her husband's child, they rarely slept together, and she always used protection.

Kiya decided to take the risk and have the baby. It was a mistake. When the doctor delivered the child, the room went silent except for the baby's cries. The little girl was brown-skinned, with coal-black hair and light brown eyes.

Her husband's joy collapsed in an instant.

"What the hell…" He glared at her.

"What the hell have you done?"

He lunged, grabbing her by the throat. The doctor and nurses pulled him away as she screamed and cried, "I'm sorry!"

He stormed out of the room and ran into her father and brothers in the hall. Seeing his face, they assumed something was wrong with the baby.

"What's wrong?" they asked.

"Your daughter just delivered a black baby. Congratulations."

"What are you talking about?" roared Master Brown as he stormed inside.

The nurse was washing the infant as Master Brown approached.

"Yes," he said coldly.

"It's definitely black."

"Why, Kiya? What were you thinking?"

"I guess the apple doesn't fall far from the tree, Daddy. I take after you, I suppose."

Master Brown slapped her across the face and walked out.

Cruse followed behind him.

Kiya and the baby were discharged the next day, and her father came to pick her up. He asked how she could bring shame to her husband and family.

"I was lonely, Daddy."

"You couldn't find a white man to ease your loneliness? It had to be a slave?"

"Daddy, you've always slept with slave girls."

"That's different. I couldn't get pregnant."

When they arrived home, she looked around for her husband and the baby's father.

"Don't bother looking for your husband. He's gone."

"Where is he, Daddy?"

"He left you. Did you expect him to stay and parade you around with this little black baby?"

Kiya called all the house slaves together, demanding to know what happened. They stood silently.

Her father barked, "Damnit! Speak up. Tell her what she asks!"

Kiya's assistant stepped forward. "When your husband returned from the hospital, his masseuse confessed what had happened between you two. He said you forced him and feared to tell. Your husband believed him because he was in love with the masseuse, and he with him. He knew the only way he'd sleep with you was if he were forced. Everyone knew of their relationship. They packed up their things and left as soon as he returned from the hospital."

"Does he know he has a child?"

"Yes, ma'am. Your husband told him."

Kiya's father laughed. "I knew something was wrong with that boy. You should have too. He spent more time with his masseuse than with you. And why would either of you think that baby was his? You never slept together."

Kiya handed the baby to her assistant. "Find a nanny."

Then she stormed upstairs to her room in tears.

Master Brown told the assistant not to worry about a nanny. "I'm sending the baby to its father. It may have been born to my daughter, but it's still a slave."

Kiya never recovered from the loss, her husband, her lover, and her baby were gone. She searched her father's office for their whereabouts but found nothing. Perhaps one day their paths would cross.

Chapter 37
To the White House

—⁓—

"Wake up! Wake up! It's all over the news!" yelled Jesse, trying to rouse Gabriel.

"What is it?"

"They discovered President Hamilton is black. It's everywhere."

"Oh no, I have to call James," Gabriel said, jumping out of bed.

"James, what's happening?"

"I don't know. I've tried reaching him, but my calls aren't going through."

James explained that everyone was in an uproar. People wondered how a black man was allowed to run for president. The controversy began when he proposed abolishing slavery. They scrutinized his background, questioning how he could pretend to be white to win votes. He had won both white voters and free blacks. Now they demanded impeachment.

The majority of the white population worried about how the United States would survive without slavery. They argued that slaves ran the country, the physical labor that kept the economy afloat, while whites reaped the benefits. Without slavery, how would they survive?

A week later, the nation was in chaos. Riots erupted across the country, mostly among white voters who felt tricked into supporting Hamilton. They claimed that if they had known he was black, they would never have voted for him.

Rioters gathered around the White House, threatening to storm it. The military was deployed to protect the president. Regardless of his race, he was sworn in as President of the United States.

The controversy stemmed from assumptions. Hamilton's father and grandfather were white U.S. Senators, and he appeared white. No one knew his mother, she died in childbirth. Yet whites dismissed all of this. To them, he was black, and a black man could not run the country. They accused him of trying to destroy it by abolishing slavery.

Gabriel and his family watched the news constantly. Rioting had escalated so much that schools were closed. Slaves were safe because they belonged to slaveowners, but free blacks were vulnerable. They were advised to stay indoors.

It was eventually announced that President Hamilton could not be impeached. He had never lied about his race, and the Constitution did not forbid a black man from running. As a free black man, he was legally safe. He would remain President of the United States until his term ended.

Gabriel jumped off the couch. "Yes!"

He hugged Jesse. "We still have a chance."

"No, we don't. This proves it. They're not going to set us free, Gabriel. They'll assassinate him first."

"Gabriel, we live in a country that's evil and greedy. This is the only country in the world that still practices slavery. These white bastards are just plain evil."

Jesse froze, looking up to see Master Kisen and Hope standing in the doorway. Fear washed over her. "Master Kisen, I'm sorry, sir."

"That's alright, Jesse. I understand how you feel. I just brought Hope over, she wanted to be with her family, and I didn't think it was safe for her to be in the streets alone."

He winked at Hope and left.

"You two always seem to meet up," Jesse said.

Before Hope could speak, her mother cut her off. "Stop. Don't say anything. I'm tired of the lies."

"Mom, I haven't lied. Please don't start. This isn't the right time. I just wanted to be with my family."

Jesse placed her hand on Hope's belly. "The time is getting close."

"Yes, it is."

Suddenly there was a special announcement on TV: "There has been an attempted assassination on President Hamilton's life. Shots were fired, but the assailant was apprehended before any casualties occurred."

Hope grabbed her mother's hand. "I told you, Dad. They'll kill him before they set us free."

Gabriel's phone rang. It was James. "I need you to come over."

"I'll be right there."

"Dad, be careful."

Chapter 38
The Underground

———∿∿∿———

When Gabriel arrived, James led him to the basement where the rest of the members were gathered. They began discussing their options. James told everyone to calm down, the President was fine, and that he had good news.

"The headquarters that controls the chips has been located," James said.

"We're planning to deactivate them. If we destroy these devices, we'll be free, free to live in the country we built."

James guided Gabriel through a hidden passage behind a closet wall. They walked down a narrow corridor to an elevator. James entered a code, then scanned his eye. The elevator descended and came to a stop.

"What is this, James? Where are we going?"

"You'll see. I want you to finally understand what we do here, how far our organization reaches."

The elevator doors opened to a large office. They crossed to a massive window overlooking a sprawling rail station.

"Welcome to the Underground Railroad, Gabriel, started in the 1800s," James said.

"Most people think Harriet Tubman started it, but it existed before her. She joined the effort in 1822 and continued until 1913."

"Why are you showing me this now?"

"Because we need you. Things aren't going as smoothly as expected, and we need your expertise to move forward."

"How do you run something this elaborate without being detected, especially with the chips inside us?"

"Detection chip?" James smiled.

"Gabriel, I don't have a detection chip. I'm free, remember? Yours only shows you're in my basement."

James explained that the slaves' devices were individually deactivated and removed before entering the facility, and cameras were temporarily blacked out so escape routes couldn't be seen. On official records, the chips appeared to malfunction for a few minutes. There were hidden locations across the United States to enter the Underground, just like train stations.

He explained that the chips had to be deactivated simultaneously nationwide to guarantee a successful takeover.

"You see, Gabriel, slaves and free blacks outnumber whites by seventy-two percent. When the chips are deactivated, how can they control us? We'll be free."

Chapter 39
Baby Arrives

A month had passed, and the country was still in turmoil. Riots continued, and another attempt on the president's life had failed. The Underground was close to completing their deactivation plans.

Because of the unrest, Hope had been staying with her parents while Kisen spent much of his time away on business.

Hope came downstairs. "Mom, I think it's time."

"Oh my God, Gabriel, it's time!" her mother yelled.

Jesse told the kids to behave, then led Hope to the car and drove to the hospital.

"Mama, call Master Kisen."

"Why? We don't need him... or do we?"

"Yes, we do, Mom."

"Why, Hope?"

"Because he's the father."

"I knew it! I knew he was the father!"

"I knew something was going on between you two. He was always around you, or maybe you were always around him."

"Jesse, calm down. Now is not the time," Gabriel said firmly.

"Why didn't you tell us?"

"I knew you would be upset."

"Did he force you?"

"No, Mom. It was consensual."

"Mom, I'm in labor, stop with the questions. Hurry, Dad!"

"You alright? Your contractions aren't close, so continue."

"Remember when I disappeared and you couldn't contact me? Kisen took me to Paris as a graduation gift."

"What?"

"Yes, Mom. It was beautiful, I walked around a free country as a free woman. I never felt anything like it."

"He made my dreams come true. He treated me so well, and we fell in love, yes Mom, we fell in love with each other."

Hope told them about their plan to move to Paris and raise their child in a free country, because Kisen didn't want his child labeled a slave. She explained that he was nothing like his father.

"Mom, he didn't choose this life, he was born into it. This is the only life he knows."

"So, if you two move to Paris, what will he do about his slaves?"

"Oh my God, Mom, it hurts!"

"Come on, baby, you can do this."

"Okay, it passed. To answer your question, he will buy us from his father and set us free."

Gabriel spoke up. "Hope, don't you see what's happening? Slavery is going to be abolished."

"Dad, it's not going to happen."

They arrived at the hospital, and Gabriel carried Hope into the emergency room.

"Dad, I can walk, and please call Kisen."

Gabriel called Kisen. "Master Kisen, Hope is in labor. She asked me to call you, and we just arrived at the hospital."

"I'll be right there."

Hope and her mother returned to the delivery room while Gabriel waited. Kisen arrived, ran past Gabriel into the delivery room without stopping, and took Hope's hand, not caring who was watching. Jesse observed, seeing their love fully for the first time, something they had hidden for months.

The doctor was getting ready to deliver the baby. "Push, Hope, push!"

After one final push, the baby arrived. "It's a boy," the doctor said, handing him to the nurse.

The nurse laid him on Hope's chest. Kisen beamed with pride. "He's beautiful," he said to Hope.

"Yes, he is," Jesse said.

"Do you have a name?"

"We are going to name him Zion."

"Zion, that's a beautiful name."

The nurse took the baby, washed him, weighed him, and handed him to Kisen. They began preparing the paperwork and asked for the father's name. Kisen said, "I'm the father," giving his full name. He then handed the baby to Jesse.

"I'll be back, I have something I need to do," he added, walking out to the waiting room. He told Gabriel, "Go on in. You have a handsome grandson," and left.

Gabriel joined his wife in the delivery room. He looked at his new grandson. "Oh my, he's a beautiful baby."

Jesse smiled at her daughter. "You two do love each other, don't you?"

"Yes, we do, Mom. I'm sorry I didn't tell you, I was afraid."

"What could I have done, Hope? He's... our Master."

"I thought you would be disappointed because I fell in love with my Master."

"I would have been disappointed if you had fallen in love with someone who didn't love you, but I see for myself that he does love you."

Chapter 40
Time for a Change

—◦◦◦—

Kisen called his lawyer. "I need to see you, and I need to see you now. It's very important."

While driving to his lawyer's office, he thought about Hope and his new son, wanting a better life for them, not the life of a slave. He had much to do. His first stop was the bank to move some money and convert part of it into Euros. His next stop was his attorney.

"I have a son," Kisen told Blake.

"I'm planning to ask his mother to marry me. She's my slave, and we're moving to Paris to raise our child. Blake, I need you to set it up; make all arrangements. I want everything to go smoothly."

"Kisen, what are you thinking?"

"That's all I've been doing, thinking, wondering if I'm doing the right thing. When I saw the birth of my son, I knew what I had to do, and I'm doing it. Blake, you and I have been friends since we were kids, you know how I feel about this slavery system. I didn't have a choice, I was born into it, but I don't have to stay in it. It's time for me to make a change, and that's what I'm doing."

"I know, Kisen, but are you going to give all this up? This is your heritage, and you know your sister and brother will flip. Your father needs you."

"I know, but I'll still run the companies. I have my inheritance, stocks, and bonds, I'm good. My family will be secure for generations. As for my father, I'll keep tabs to make sure my siblings are handling things properly."

"What about your slaves?"

"If it were up to me, I'd set them all free. I can at least set mine free."

"You're what? Are you crazy? Sell them."

"I can't. I was going to sell them to my brother and sister, but I wouldn't do that to them. Don't you see how my siblings treat their slaves? I wouldn't do that to them."

"Your siblings will be furious. These slaves are your family's heritage, they've been in your family for generations."

"I know, but they're mine, and I can do what I want with my property."

"You're right, they're yours."

"Just get it started, Blake. I'll provide details. I'm keeping my part of the plantation and my house. I want to move some money overseas, prepare the release of my slaves, arrange reparations, and ensure organizations help them transition."

"Okay, I'll get started. But shouldn't you talk to your father and siblings first?"

"My father's Alzheimer's has worsened. I'll talk to my siblings. Also, I need Gabriel's family freed immediately. I'll send you my son's birth certificate so you can take care of Hope and Zion."

"I'll meet with my brother and sister and tell them your plans. Wish me luck."

Kisen called his sister and told her to meet him at their father's house as soon as possible.

He arrived at the house at the same time as Kiya, and they went in together. He told them of his plans to marry Hope, move to Paris to raise their child in a free country, and set his slaves free.

Cruse was furious, as Kisen expected, especially about him freeing his slaves.

"Have you lost your mind? These slaves belong to our family, they're not just yours. They were our father's, our grandfather's, our great-grandfather's. How can you set them free? If you don't want them, then give them to us or sell them to us. It's not right, Kisen."

"I will not turn them over to you."

"If you want to marry your slave and move away, go ahead, but these slaves belong to this plantation, our plantation."

"Like I said, I'm not turning them over to you. They're my slaves to do what I want, and this is what I choose to do."

"Didn't you learn anything from our father? He trusted you to carry on our legacy, not destroy it. He would be so disappointed with you."

"Then go tell him."

His sister began to cry. "How could you do this to us, Kisen? Dad put you in charge."

"I'm not giving up on our companies. I'll still take care of the businesses from Paris. You and Carson need to step up and take running this plantation seriously."

"What about you marrying a slave, Kisen?" his sister asked.

"I love her."

"Oh my God!" she yelled.

"Didn't you fall in love with one, sis? Didn't you have a kid, or have you forgotten?"

She ran out of the room. "Don't run," Kisen called after her. Cruse stepped into Kisen's face.

"I won't let you do this."

"You can't stop me."

"If Father knew you'd do this, he would have never given them to you."

"I know," Kisen said as he walked out.

The house slaves overheard the conversation between Kisen and his siblings. The news spread fast among the slaves on the plantation. Some of Kisen's slaves were happy about being free, but some were afraid, especially the older ones. They had always been taken care of and didn't know how to survive freedom or care for themselves. The news was received with mixed feelings.

Chapter 41
The Day of Emancipation

A week passed, and the emancipation papers had been signed. Kisen was picking up Hope and Zion and heading to the plantation to meet with all his slaves.

He arrived at the plantation where everyone was gathered. Before he walked up to the podium, he handed Hope and Zion their emancipation papers.

"Surprise. You are free, baby, free to do anything you want, go anywhere you want, and be with whomever you want."

She started to cry. "Thank you, baby. You know I choose to go where you go. I choose you."

Kisen called Gabriel to the stage and handed him his family's papers. Jesse began to cry. "Thank you, sir."

Destinee hugged him. "Thank you, Master Kisen."

"Sweetheart, I'm no longer your Master. Call me Kisen."

"Thank you, Kisen."

He then motioned for Mercy and her mother, handing them their papers. Mercy hugged him. "Thank you, Master, sir, I mean Kisen."

They both laughed.

He walked to the edge of the stage. "Hello everyone. I know you're wondering what this is about, and some of you already know. You and your ancestors have been a part of this plantation for over 200 years. You were my legacy, a legacy I was born into, but I'm ready to give it up. Therefore, I'm granting you your freedom."

The room went silent, then low whispers began, followed by cheers, crying, tears of joy, and some sadness. He heard the fear in some of them.

"I know some of you are worried. This is the only life you've ever known. But don't worry, I'm not going to throw you to the wolves. It will be a tough adjustment, but I've set you up with the local freeman's organization to help you transition. I'll pass out their information along with your emancipation papers. Those of you who live on the plantation have six months to move unless you have jobs here.

"The only difference is, instead of giving me half your money, it's all yours now, along with the jobs you have. Those of you working here will continue drawing a check from me for six months, or until you find employment, which the organization will help you with.

"I've talked to my brother and sister, so you won't be bothered by them. If you are, you'll have my number. "You'll be alright. Enjoy your freedom."

Everyone began to clap. They cheered for him, thanked him. The cheers continued as Kisen and Hope drove off.

He made a stop at the house and went to his study. Sitting at his desk, he pulled out the device that monitored his slaves and deactivated it. He sat for a few minutes, thinking. Then he got up, returned with a hammer, and began smashing it so it could never be used again.

His butler stood in the doorway watching. "Are you done, sir?"

Kisen looked up and began to laugh. "Yes, I'm done."

"I'm going to miss you, sir."

"I'm going to miss you too, and thank you for taking care of me all these years, even though you didn't have a choice."

"Sir, I've enjoyed taking care of you, watching you grow into the man you are, a good man. Make sure you keep in touch. You have my number, and keep an eye on my siblings for me. Let me know if they start acting stupid."

"I sure will, sir."

Kisen went out to the car and took Hope by the hand. "Now I'm no longer a slave owner."

"Let's go home," he said as they made their way to the airport.

Chapter 42
Deactivation

—∿—

The country is still rioting over the President's push to abolish slavery. Everyone is glued to the TV, waiting to see if the bill makes its way through Congress. The room grows silent as the announcement comes: it did not pass. Slavery still exists. The whole white population is celebrating. On the news, an older white woman is interviewed.

"Our country is saved, now get that nigger out of the White House."

Gabriel looks at Jesse. "This was all for nothing. All the work we've done to get President Hamilton in office."

"We could move to Paris with Kisen and Hope. They did invite us," replies Jesse.

"This is our home, Jesse. Do you really want to leave it?"

"Yes, I do. Hope told me how we would be treated there, like human beings instead of property."

"But we are free, babe."

"But look how we're treated. We're still treated like slaves, not equals. We will never be equal."

Gabriel begins thinking about the other option. He starts to smile.

"We have something else in the works. It may still happen."

"What is it?" asks Jesse.

"I can't talk about it. You know that. You just have to trust me."

"I'll be back. I have to run to James."

Gabriel arrives at James's to talk about preparations for the alternate plan. They've already devised a way to gain entrance to the facility, which is operated by slaves, people they have on the inside will help

160

them get in. Once they're inside, that's where Gabriel steps in. He's needed to break the code.

Gabriel leaves James's house with a briefcase filled with critical information that will help him break the code to destroy the chips. He spends days working on it, on breaks at work, late at night, falling asleep at his desk. He finally succeeds. He runs to Jesse and wakes her.

"Babe, I did it!"

"Oh my God. Are you going to call James?"

"No, I'll wait until morning. I don't want to tell him over the phone."

Gabriel is too excited to sleep, so he and Jesse spend the night talking about the future. They love the fact that they're free, but to be free in a country where slavery still exists brings its own restrictions because of the color of your skin. There are still places you can't go or things you can't do. Your children can't play on playgrounds with white kids. You can't even wear what you want, it has to be a certain color to distinguish the type of slave you are. This is not freedom.

Morning finally arrives. Gabriel can't wait to get to work to tell James the good news, but James isn't at work. This isn't like him, he's usually the first one in the office. Something isn't right. Gabriel leaves and drives to James's house. It's surrounded by police and the FBI. They're everywhere. He sees them putting James, handcuffed, into the back of a car.

Gabriel's phone rings. It's one of the Underground members.

"Check your coded messages," is all he says.

Gabriel immediately decodes the message: You have a package taped under your desk drawer.

Gabriel returns to his office to retrieve the package. James's office is occupied by the FBI, who are going through his computer. Gabriel thinks, They won't find anything. James has been involved in the Underground his whole life, he's too smart to leave anything on his work computer. He's still wondering what tipped them off.

Gabriel finds the package and slips it into his briefcase. He doesn't feel it's safe to open at work. He finishes his day without interacting with anyone. A few coworkers ask what's going on with James, everyone knows they're friends, but Gabriel just stays to himself and finishes his workday. He can't wait to go home to see what's in the package.

The day finally ends. Gabriel wants to check the package in the work garage but decides it's not wise. He waits until he's home. He's not used to arriving at an empty house, but since they acquired their freedom, the kids take their time getting home. He goes to his office and slowly opens the package. Inside, he finds a flash drive from James.

Gabriel, if you're reading this, it means I've been arrested. It doesn't mean our plans are over. I still need you to proceed. Inside this package you will find an airline ticket that will take you to Salt Lake City. When you arrive, someone will pick you up at the airport. They'll take you to where you will meet with the team you'll be working with. You will destroy the facility that controls the towers, which will disarm the chips. We will be free. Don't worry about me, they won't find anything. This isn't the first time they've investigated me. I'll see you soon. Good luck. I have faith in you.

Gabriel didn't have a chance to tell James that he broke the code. This means the operation will be completed sooner than they expected. James had already covered everything at work for Gabriel to take this trip, prior to being detained. The cover for his family was that he was taking a business trip. He didn't think it would be safe to tell his wife the truth. No one must know.

Gabriel arrives at the airport. Being Black, he has an enormous amount of documentation to prove he's free, photo ID, Emancipation papers, proof of chip removal. He finally gains access to his flight. He's nervous, he's never flown before.

As he walks down the aisle to the back of the plane, where the Blacks are seated, he receives glares from the white passengers as if to say, I dare you be free. He observes a couple of smiles, but only a couple. He's using his newfound freedom to look them in the eyes, something he wasn't allowed to do as a slave, and they hate it.

He makes his way to the back and notices they're occupied by three black men and a woman. He feels a little better knowing he's not the only Black person on the plane. He tries to hide his nervousness, like he's flown before, but when the engine starts up Gabriel almost jumps out of his seat.

The man next to him laughs. "Gabriel, you're not alone; none of us have flown before. We're all scared shitless."

"How do you know my name?"

"We're all going to the same place. We're part of your team. I'm Devin."

"Nice to meet you, Devin."

"I'll introduce you to the rest of the team when we land. Just relax, Gabriel, this is about a four-hour flight. Get some sleep. We have a lot to do and little time."

The plane rolls down the runway. Gabriel watches as they take off, the pressure pushes him back in his seat. He's amazed at the clouds and how small everything looks below. He thought he would never see this, that it was only a privilege for white people or the lucky few Blacks who traveled with their Masters, but here he is. The only time he'd left Washington, D.C., was to visit his daughter at the university, and that wasn't very far. Now he's headed to the other side of the country.

He notices Devin is knocked out and decides to try, but the scenery is too beautiful. He takes a few pictures on his phone, though the camera can't capture it. He finally dozes off after a couple of hours.

Everyone is jarred awake by the landing. Devin smiles. "We made it in one piece."

They load into a van, Devin introduces Gabriel to the team and fills him in on the plans. They drive into the desert for about an hour until they reach a canyon wall. The rock opens and the van enters. A woman meets them as they exit.

"Hello, everyone. My name is Candace. Follow me."

They're led into a classroom already occupied by several team members and take seats as instructed for the briefing. Candace welcomes everyone to the Cave, that's what this facility is called, and introduces James, head of the Underground. Gabriel practically jumps from his seat, he had no idea he'd see James again.

James explains he was briefly detained by the FBI but released for lack of evidence. He then outlines the mission and each team's tasks: the group will split into two, a technicians' team led by Gabriel, responsible for gaining entrance, and a militia that will set the bombs once inside and eliminate anyone who interferes. "This is war," he says.

Once the facility is destroyed, the towers and chips will shut down and the controllers will lose power over the slaves. "They won't control us anymore. We occupy seventy-five percent of the population, how can they control us? Tomorrow we will be free." Meeting adjourned.

James walks over to Gabriel and asks, "Are you ready?"

"Yes. I'm ready. I broke the code."

"That's great. That cuts a lot of time, we can practically walk in."

"Good work, Gabriel. Now go to your room and get some sleep. Morning will sneak up on you, and you need to be ready."

Morning arrives. Training starts after breakfast and lasts most of the day. When it's completed everyone changes into black gear to blend into the night. Before departing they're told to call their families but say nothing. Gabriel calls Jesse and the kids, tells them not to worry, that he'll be home and that he loves them, then hangs up.

They load into two eighteen-wheelers; one for the team, the other for equipment, and are scheduled to arrive in about two hours, at sunset, so the night will hide them. The vehicles stop about a mile from the facility. They exit and begin the last mile on foot. In the distance they see the facility lights. Gabriel is told to hold back with his team until he receives a call to proceed, the tactical team goes first. Suddenly the lights around the facility go out. Then Gabriel gets the call: proceed with caution.

At the facility they find all the security guards captured without casualties and the workers rounded up. They hadn't known whether there'd be resistance since the place is run by government-owned slaves. Gabriel's team is led to the hostages, he's instructed to tell them what's about to happen. When he finishes they cheer and offer their help. They also say they must hurry because the men in charge, who are white, will be back first thing in the morning.

Gabriel explained there was nothing to worry about, the facility would be detonated before anyone arrived. One of the workers asked, "What do we do afterward? We belong to the government."

"Anything you want. The transition won't be easy, but you will be free," Gabriel replied.

The explosives were set throughout the facility, and everyone prepared to leave. They would be detonated once they reached the trailers. The guards and technicians protested.

"We can't. They'll think we did this."

Gabriel led them away and tied them up. "They won't think you're part of it now. You can tell them what happened, they'll know anyway. Take care of yourselves."

Gabriel reached for the panel, said a prayer, and pressed the button. The explosion lit up the sky, visible for miles, as the trailers drove off. The chips were simultaneously deactivated, though no one knew it yet. Suddenly, a pre-recorded broadcast took over the airwaves across the United States. Gabriel turned on the TV in the back of the trailer so the men could watch.

A black man, dressed in black with his face covered by a mask, began to speak:

"My brothers and sisters, I am a member of the Underground. I am here to tell you your bondage is over. You are free, free to live as you choose. The chips in your bodies that kept you in bondage have been permanently destroyed. The facility that controlled them has been destroyed. Don't be afraid. I know this transition will be challenging, but we will do this together. Take to the streets, let's celebrate. Celebrate our freedom. We are free."

Suddenly, it was like an explosion. The streets filled with Black people celebrating across the United States. People danced through the cities, but the celebration quickly turned to violence, whites were beaten, some killed, windows broken, buildings burned, cars torched. Everything spiraled out of control.

The police, who were government-owned slaves and now free, were in the streets celebrating too. There was no one to control the violence.

It went on for days. Then, suddenly, the President took to the airways to make a special announcement.

Hear me, brothers and sisters. I am coming to you tonight to ask for your help. I am desperately searching for something that seems lost. Only you can help me find it. My fear is that if I do not find it soon, my house will crumble.

Look closely at your television screen. I am holding up two pictures. In my left hand, you see a picture of people lying on the ground. If you look closely, you can see that they have been murdered. What is not obvious to the naked eye is that these are some of my family members. They dared to dream of a day when we would be free. They had the audacity to risk everything, teaching us to read by candlelight late at night, just as the daughter of one of their ancestors' owners had taught them.

In my right hand is a second picture. Here you see people smiling. You probably cannot see that they are pouring with sweat. Their eyes, though sparkling, cannot hide that they are exhausted, tired and sweaty, yet smiling. Why? Because they overcame everything the day threw at them and survived. The indignities they faced drained their energy, but could not rob them of their determination to succeed. Against all odds, they persevered. Why? Because their vision of freedom was stronger than anything slavery had to offer.

The people in both pictures, those smiling and those who lay dead, had something in common. They all had dreams and visions of freedom for their people. Although they likely realized they would not see it themselves, their sacrifice was not in vain. Their faith was unwavering, believing that their commitment to a vision of a free society would come to pass for their descendants.

Brothers and sisters, I am searching for the vision they dreamed about. My heart tells me it is near, but it is being clouded by the lawlessness I see in our streets tonight. The violence, the thirst for vengeance, and the disregard for human life when it comes in white skin are blocking the promised land. I implore you to stop what you are doing in the streets. We have all waited generations to be free of the chips that dehumanized us. Our wait was for a destiny that will place us on the throne of leadership rather than in the alley of despair.

Stop what you are doing in the streets and honor the sacrifice that your ancestors and mine made.

I beg you to help me find what will surely be lost if this continues. If your actions help us discover what seems to be fading, then we will triumph together. As your leader, I make this request of you. What will you do with it?

Suddenly the violence stops as fast as it started. The President made sense, we built this country with our hands, our blood, sweat, and tears, why should we destroy it. We are civilized, we are not animals. The world is watching us, let them know that we deserve this new found freedom. We have to live with the very people who put us in bondage.

Chapter 43
Freedom

Over the past year, blacks had to train whites how to survive without them. This meant going to work and learning to fend for themselves. Whites had to go to school to learn the tasks the slaves had been doing for them. Of course, there were wealthy whites who had grown rich off the backs of slaves, they were fine. But those who hadn't had that advantage now had to work for a living.

A year has passed. It's Thanksgiving Day. Kisen and Hope have just landed at the airport. They haven't been back since leaving for Paris a year ago. As they walk through the airport with their baby girl, they notice how different things are, blacks and whites working side by side.

Gabriel picks them up at the airport. He hugs Hope and his granddaughter. Kisen holds out his hand to shake, but Gabriel looks him in the eye, a gesture he had never made. Kisen slaps his hand down and embraces him. Gabriel feels uncomfortable but hugs him back.

While driving home, Kisen asks to make a detour to the plantation. They pass through the gate by his father's house. The plantation looks empty without the slaves. Only a few stayed, older ones content, or too afraid to start a new life.

Kisen stops at his sister's house and rings the doorbell. The butler, who decided to stay, opens the door. His sister walks in, sees Kisen, and runs to hug him.

"I missed you so much."

"I missed you too, little sister."

He notices a little girl, a beautiful, hazel-eyed biracial girl.

"Is that who I think it is?"

"Yes, Kisen. It's my little girl. When slavery was abolished, her father brought her to me."

"I'm happy for you, sis. How's our little brother doing?"

"Not well, he's had a hard time adjusting, but he'll be alright. It'll just take a little longer."

"And father?"

"As well as can be expected. He doesn't know us, so of course he won't know you."

Kisen tells her he'll return tomorrow with his family. "I'm so proud of you, sis. I see the change in you."

"She did it," she says, pointing at her daughter.

Gabriel arrives at the house. Hope notices her parents have moved to a new neighborhood into a much larger home.

"Dad, you have a new house."

"Yes, we needed more space."

Inside, Jesse greets them warmly, hugging and kissing her daughter and granddaughter. She walks up to Kisen, hugs him, and kisses his cheek. She whispers something she has never said before:

"Thank you for everything you've done for my family."

"It's a pleasure."

Destinee, Mercy, and Samuel hear them, run downstairs, and greet everyone with hugs and kisses. Suddenly, there's a knock at the door. Gabriel opens it, it's Claudette, Mercy's mother, come for Thanksgiving dinner. She hugs Kisen and thanks him for everything he's done for her and her daughter. The room fills with love.

Suddenly, a Special Announcement from the President appears on the TV. Everyone stops and turns toward it.

Good afternoon. I would like to wish each of you a very Happy Thanksgiving. This is a time of celebration. It is a time for family. It is a time for us, as U.S. citizens, to take stock of how far we have come. Please know that I am deeply honored to serve as your President.

It has been a year since we joined other nations around the world in becoming a country of free men and women, regardless of their skin color or ethnic background. Although we were last to reach this milestone, it does not diminish the significance of our humanitarian achievement. Now that we are working as truly one nation, we are poised to unlock the possibilities of our combined efforts to elevate our country. Scores of people have died, and many have lived longing for the day when we could truthfully say the United States of America has become a single nation of inclusivity.

When our families gather at Thanksgiving, we not only enjoy great food together, but we also remember those who provided the foundation of what we have become. No matter how much time has passed, during this particular celebration our hearts are reminded of our bloodline. Our memories of them bring a smile to our faces and a tear to the corner of our eyes.

As we approach this holiday, I have given much thought to the steps we can take as a nation to mark where we have been and where we are going. I felt we needed to blend symbolism and substance. Our being a free nation comes as a result of blending all of our people into a unified mosaic. Some might say that I stand as a symbol of this blending because of my heritage, being the offspring of a white mother and a Black father.

My fellow citizens, I am pleased to announce that right after this holiday season, I will be proposing to Congress that we make the necessary investments to create a new example of America's greatness. I expect this to be an attraction that will draw people from around the country. This place will be spread over several hundred acres and will be known simply as The Promised Land.

As you enter, the first section will be referred to as Grace Grove. In Grace Grove, we will plant species of trees that were prevalent during all the centuries when we enslaved our Black brothers and sisters. In the center of these trees will stand a flower garden comprised of species that represent the various cultures found in our country. Although we have a dark past, we have a bright future. Those who come to visit may be overcome with grief, anger, or other emotions. Regardless of what you bring with you, this place will stand as a reminder that we are called to extend grace to those around us. None of us are perfect. But working together, we can move closer to perfection if we extend and accept grace.

In one corner of Grace Grove will be a small gravesite, known as the Cemetery of Isms. Here, headstones will read "Racism," "Sexism," and "Ageism." These headstones will symbolize that, at last, we are laying to rest the things that have kept us from our promise of greatness as a nation. It is my hope that Grace Grove will be a place of redemption and renewal for all who visit.

As you move out of Grace Grove, you will see a magnificent campus dedicated to innovation. It will be called Joint Vision University. On this campus, Black and White employees will work side by side to invent things that will propel the United States to new heights of global competitiveness. Symbolism and substance, that will be the hallmark of The Promised Land. I hope Congress will support my proposal.

Fellow citizens, Happy Thanksgiving. Thank you for all you have done to bring us forward. We can now move ahead as a proud member of the United Nations, for at long last, we are truly One Nation Under God. Enjoy your holiday.

www.ingramcontent.com/pod-product-compliance
Lightning Source LLC
Chambersburg PA
CBHW030254130626
46549CB00002B/521